NEW
ORK
AT
CHOOL

HASE

UBLIC
ICATION
ASS'N

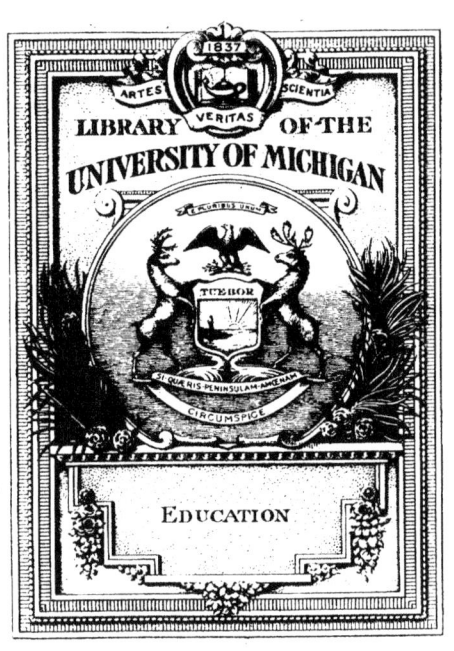

LA
339
.N5
C49

NEW YORK AT SCHOOL

NEW YORK AT SCHOOL

A Description of the Activities
and Administration of the Public Schools
of the City of New York

BY

JOSEPHINE CHASE
Assistant Director, Public Education Association

IN COLLABORATION WITH

THE SCHOOL AUTHORITIES

PUBLIC EDUCATION ASSOCIATION
OF THE CITY OF NEW YORK

1927

COPYRIGHT, 1927, BY PUBLIC EDUCATION ASSOCIATION

COMMONWEALTH PRESS   WORCESTER, MASS.

FOREWORD

THIS story of *New York at School* has been designed to further the purpose of the Public Education Association to inform its members and citizens generally of the work of the City schools. For years, the Association has discussed various educational questions of current interest in its bulletins and in articles in the public press. This is the first time, however, that an effort has been made to present a comprehensive picture of the school system as a whole, in order that the average citizen might see its numerous activities in relation to one another. The Association has long contemplated the publication of such an account, but until this year has found it impossible to spare any one of its staff to do the painstaking work involved.

The aim of the book is to describe the work of the schools in a non-critical way, without any attempt at appraisal, by sketching briefly the origin of the several activities, the way in which they are being carried on, and the objectives which the school authorities have in view. In order that this might be accurately done, the coöperation and assistance of the superintendents and specialists in the school system was enlisted from the very beginning. The fact that it is a description of the work of the schools from the point of view of those who are actually carrying it on, rather than an interpretation solely from our own viewpoint, is evident from the following list of individuals, and those cited elsewhere, who either furnished material or approved the text after its completion.

FOREWORD

Among those who aided in planning and organizing the book, we are particularly obligated to: Dr. Eugene Nifenecker, Director of the Division of Reference, Research and Statistics; Dr. John S. Roberts, Assistant to the Superintendent of Schools; Dr. Louis Marks of the Board of Examiners; Morris Siegel, Director of Continuation and Evening Schools; George Chatfield, Assistant Director of the Bureau of Attendance; Frank A. Rexford, Supervisor of Civics in the High Schools; and District Superintendents William E. Grady and Stephen F. Bayne.

The plan for the book was approved by Dr. William J. O'Shea, Superintendent of Schools, before the manuscript was prepared. With his permission, the aid of those in charge of the special fields of school work was obtained in gathering the data and checking up the final manuscript for accuracy. The School Visiting Committee of the Women's City Club, with the aid of members of the Junior League, under the Chairmanship of Mrs. Samuel A. Lewisohn, rendered special aid in making available the data gathered in the course of their visits to a large number of the public schools of the City.

After the manuscript had been completed and had been checked by the specialists in the school system, it was carefully read by District Superintendent T. Adrian Curtis, at the request of the Superintendent of Schools, and was approved for publication both by the Superintendent and by Dr. Roberts.

As is pointed out in the opening pages, it is impossible to give a perspective of the work of the schools as a whole and at the same time delve too minutely into details. Because of this, the volume must not be looked upon as an encyclopaedia, but rather as a guide book to tempt those who may be interested in certain phases of the work of the schools to seek for further details in the official reports and records of the Board of Education and to visit the schools themselves.

Those who may be interested in a more intensive study of any phase of the work of the schools will find, as we have, that the school authorities are only too willing to aid them in every way. Visitors are always welcome and need only make a request to the Superintendent of Schools for permission to visit any part of the school system. The Bureau of Reference, Research and Statistics of the Board of Education, to which we are particularly grateful for constant assistance in gathering data, is especially equipped and willing to be of service. It is our hope that we may be able to re-issue this story from time to time, so amended as to bring the material up to date.

HOWARD W. NUDD, Director.

June, 1927.

ACKNOWLEDGMENTS

IN addition to the special acknowledgments carried in the Foreword, the Association wishes to express its appreciation of the coöperation of the following school officials who have aided either in furnishing the original data or in verifying the accuracy of those portions of the final manuscript which deal with their respective fields of work:

Miss AGNES V. BIRMINGHAM
    Acting Director of Speech Improvement

Miss MAUDE J. BLEIER
    Manager of School Lunches

Dr. J. L. BLUMENTHAL
    Director of the Bureau of Child Hygiene of the Board of Health

GEORGE B. BUCK
    Actuary of the Teachers' Retirement System

Dr. HAROLD G. CAMPBELL
    Associate Superintendent in charge of High Schools

FREDERICK G. CHAMBERS
    Auditor of the Bureau of Finance

Dr. FRANCES COHEN
    Assistant Director of Educational Hygiene

FRANK H. COLLINS
    Director of Art and Drawing

ERNEST L. CRANDALL
    Director of the Bureau of Lectures

THOMAS DONOHUE
    Principal, Parental School

Miss SARAH ELKUS
    Supervisor of Continuation Classes

Miss HENRIETTA FLAMM
    Division of Reference, Research and Statistics

Miss ELIZABETH FARRELL
    Inspector of Ungraded Classes

GEORGE G. GARTLAN
    Director of Music

EUGENE C. GIBNEY
    Director of Extension Activities

WILLIAM GOMPERT
    Superintendent of School Buildings

FOREST GRANT
    Director of Art in High Schools

Dr. WILLIAM A. HANNIG
    Chairman of the Board of Examiners

Miss RITA HOCHHEIMER
    Assistant Director of Visual Instruction

WILLIAM E. HORNE
    Parental School

Miss MINNIE L. HUTCHINSON
    Director of Sewing

Miss OLIVE JONES
    Principal, P. S. 120, Manhattan

PATRICK JONES
    Superintendent of School Supplies

Miss CARRIE KEARNS
    Principal, School for the Deaf

Dr. FRANKLIN J. KELLER
    Principal, East Side Continuation School

VAN EVRIE KILPATRICK
    Assigned to the supervision of School Gardens

ACKNOWLEDGMENTS

CLAUDE G. LELAND
Superintendent of Libraries

GEORGE J. LOEWY
Director of Vocational Activities

Miss JESSIE LOUDERBACK
President of the Association of Visiting Teachers

Dr. CHARLES W. LYON
Associate Superintendent in charge of Leaves of Absence for Teachers

EDWARD MANDEL
Associate Superintendent in charge of Organization of Classes in Elementary School

WILLIAM J. MCAULIFFE
Assistant Director of Extension Activities

MISS MARGARET J. MCCOOEY
Associate Superintendent in charge of Special Schools and Classes for the Handicapped and the Problem Children

Dr. WILLIAM J. MCGRATH
Assistant Director of the Bureau of Reference, Research and Statistics

JOSEPH MILLER
Secretary of the Board of Education

Miss FRANCES E. MOSCRIP
Inspector of Classes for the Blind and Sight Conservation Classes

Miss LUELLA A. PALMER
Director of Kindergartens

R. W. RODMAN
Superintendent of the Bureau of Plant Operation

Miss CAROLINA G. RONZONE
Inspector of Industrial and Placement Work for Handicapped Children

Miss CHRISTINE SCHLENKER
Principal, P. S. 61, Brooklyn

JOSEPH SHEEHAN
Associate Superintendent in charge of Physical Training

Dr. EDWARD W. STITT
Associate Superintendent in charge of Vocational Schools

Dr. ADELA J. SMITH
Assistant Director of Physical Training in charge of Handicapped Classes

Dr. GUSTAVE STRAUBENMÜLLER
Associate Superintendent in charge of Character Education

Dr. JOHN L. TILDSLEY
District Superintendent in charge of High Schools

Dr. BENJAMIN VEIT
District Superintendent in charge of Junior High Schools

Dr. A. P. WAY
Acting Director of Physical Training

Miss MARTHA WESTFALL
Director of Home-making

HERMAN W. WRIGHT
Director of High School Organization

TABLE OF CONTENTS

		Page
FOREWORD AND ACKNOWLEDGMENTS		v
PROBLEMS AND PURPOSES		1
I.	REGULAR PATHS OF SCHOOL PROGRESS	5
	1. In the Kindergartens	7
	2. In the Elementary Schools	12
	3. In the Junior High Schools	38
	4. In the High Schools	51
	5. In the Vocational Schools	70
II.	GENERAL SERVICES AFFORDED	77
	1. Health and Physical Education	79
	2. Character Education	99
	3. Visiting Teachers	104
	4. School Lunches	113
III.	SPECIAL SERVICES AFFORDED	117
	1. Classes for Physically Handicapped Children	119
	2. The Ungraded Class Department	137
	3. Special Schools for Behavior Problems	146
	Probationary Schools	146
	Adjustment Schools	149
	Detention Schools	151
	The Parental School	153
IV.	EXTENDED PATHS AND BY PATHS	157
	1. Vacation Schools	159

TABLE OF CONTENTS

    2. Continuation Schools 162
    3. Evening Schools 174
    4. Adult Education in Day Classes 180
    5. Extended Use of School Facilities 184
        Bureau of Lectures 184
        Community and Recreational Centers . 187
        Meetings and Forums 189
        Playgrounds, Swimming Pools and Showers 190

V. KEEPING TRACK OF A MILLION CHILDREN . . 193

VI. THE TEACHERS OF A MILLION CHILDREN . . . 203
    1. How New York Trains its Teachers . . . 205
    2. Examining and Promoting Teachers . . . 211
    3. Opportunities for Teachers in Service . . . 218

VII. ADMINISTERING THE SCHOOLS 223
    1. Overhead Control of Education 225
        How the State Controls the Schools . . 225
        How the City Controls the Schools . . 228
    2. Internal Administration of the Schools . . 237
    3. Business Administration of the Schools . . 249
        Making the Annual Budget and Securing Funds 249
        Auditing Accounts 255
        Erecting Buildings 256
        Operating Buildings 260
        Supplying the Schools 261

INDEX 265

PROBLEMS AND PURPOSES

THAT the New York City school system must be different from other school systems is evident from its size alone. One million pupils—more than in Chicago, St. Louis, Detroit, Boston, and Baltimore combined—762 school units, the teaching force itself larger than the entire population in more than two-thirds of the cities in New York State and larger than in any city in some states. Unusual, too, are the crowded conditions that cause many New York schools to be built up in the air six or seven stories from the midst of a city block with no grounds roundabout. The problem of teaching in a city so widespread that many children have never seen a cow, a chicken or a pig, nor any spread of growing things outside of a city park, presents peculiar difficulties. In variety of population, in assortment of races and degrees of culture, New York is unequalled.

Although the minimum essentials of education are carefully prescribed and standardized so that no school shall fall short of them, nevertheless the schools of the city show great variation not only in physical surroundings but in ways of doing things and in the mental attitudes of those in charge. It is perhaps fortunate that this is so. For in the midst of lower Manhattan where there are three or four thousand children to a school and almost every available corner accommodates a child, and in P. S. 81 Bronx, a beautiful new building with less than 400 pupils, where the children may pick violets on the school lawn and eat luncheon under the trees, the task of the teacher is necessarily different. Method of presentation and subject matter, too, must differ for children from homes where no English is spoken and for those from homes where careful parents watch over-anxiously to see that Isadore or Isabel does his or her homework.

The great task of modern schools, recognized by educators, is to give to all children the kind of education that will best meet individual needs and interests. It used to be customary to set for whole groups of children the same standards of achievement. And in a city of such bewildering size as this—the equivalent of five large school systems under the supervision of one central office—the tendency naturally was to make the physical task of administration easier by requiring all children to do the same work in the same way at the same time. But experience has taught that one set of standards will not serve for 1,000,000 children, whose talents, tastes and potential possibilities are all different.

It is to the task of individualizing education, of making the school program elastic enough to fit the needs of each child, then, that the progressive school leaders of New York are bending every effort. A gigantic task it is! How are they going to take these curiously assorted groups of children spread over so wide an area, being taught under such different conditions, often in schools with so large a register that the influence of personal contact and interest must of necessity be minimized, and give them, not some standardized brand of school but a number of individual brands?

Yet, as leaders of insight recognize, the very size and complexity of the city's school system offers the greatest possible opportunity for allowing to each child the particular work that will interest him and that will offer him the best chance for future usefulness. The system is so large, the needs of the pupils so varied, that schooling in widely different fields becomes possible. Opportunity for industrial training, for art work, for highly specialized academic work are practicable in a city where a sufficiently large group will benefit by that training. A smaller city might not be able to afford courses in brick laying, in art metal work, in clay modeling, in Italian, in office practice.

Recognizing this opportunity, the wisest school people for the last twenty or thirty years have been directing every new development, every revision of courses of study, to give to each individual child as much information, as much skill or as much curiosity as he is able to acquire.

The school program is being adjusted, first, to varying mental abilities. Children are being classified and taught in fairly homogeneous groups. Second, schools are making adjustments to further the proper physical development of pupils. Health and physical education play a large part in any school curriculum. Medical and dental supervision are used to guide the individual child in protection of his physical well being. In case a child has certain defects the school course is changed and adapted to fit the child's need and to counteract the ill effects those defects might have on his future career. Special classes are provided for seriously handicapped children.

While schools are just beginning to take into consideration a child's personality and emotional development in determining the kind of education best suited to him, they are making a real effort to offer in school the knowledge, inspiration and training that will make for the development of sturdy character.

For the schools aim, first, to give a rounded education, developing mind and body and personality; and, second, to give every child a chance before he leaves school to develop special talents and tastes, to get the particular type of education—trade, commercial, academic, artistic,—that will best fit him for a happy and useful life.

It might almost seem that these two aims are contradictory—a rounded education and a specialized education. And perhaps they are—two contradictory purposes forcing educators to find a golden mean.

In view of the foregoing considerations, it is, therefore, very hard to generalize about New York City schools—hard to give any complete picture of this huge and complex system that has inevitably grown up in somewhat haphazard fashion. The statistics cited are subject, of course, to constant change in detail, but they will serve to indicate the relative cost and size of various activities and to suggest the emphasis put upon them by the city educators. An attempt is made here only to suggest the scope of activities the schools have undertaken and to explain briefly how they grew and where they seem to be going.

I. REGULAR PATHS OF SCHOOL PROGRESS

I. IN THE KINDERGARTENS

THE story of what the New York City schools are doing for the children begins properly enough with the kindergartens. There are very few schools now where there are enough children of kindergarten age—four and a half to six years—that do not have a kindergarten. In a few over-crowded schools there is not room.

What the Kindergartens Do

The kindergarten period, more than any other part of school life, perhaps, gives the individual child a chance to be happy and successful. Its function is to introduce children naturally and gradually to school life, giving them certain fundamental information and certain necessary skill with their hands, and guiding them in the formation of useful habits.

They go for a walk and see the policeman. They go back to school and with blocks lay out the street they have just walked through. Then Antony or Mary plays policeman, directing the traffic,—a street car made with empty spools for wheels and a bus that used to be a biscuit box. Through this observation and dramatization they are learning many things, about transportation, about safety, about necessary rules of conduct, about life in a community. They go to the park, then talk and sing for days about the trees and birds, the lake and the swans, the animals of the zoo, and all the natural wonders many have never known before.

The kindergartners of the city have laid down certain standards—standards of information, of music, of art, of handwork, of language expression, of courteous and responsible relations to others—that all kindergarten children should attain. In some districts the kindergarten teacher must first teach the language and elementary habits of behavior. In outlying districts where things are not too crowded the pupils make their own gardens in a corner of the playground; in one Staten Island school the children in spring see father and mother birds building their nests and watch for the first peep of the baby birds; while in downtown Manhattan and Brooklyn a window box and pictures must suggest gardens and springtime.

Kindergarten Development

It has been fifty years since the first New York kindergarten supported by public funds was established at the Normal School, now Hunter College. But it was not until the 1890's that the school system accepted the demonstrations of model schools and established its first kindergartens. There are now 973 kindergartens in the city and 106 kindergarten extension classes, with a register of 41,613 in the regular kindergartens and 4,240 in the extension classes.

In addition to the kindergartens in school buildings there are 39 classes in annexes in day nurseries and settlement houses. In these annexes children of kindergarten age are kept all day by the nursery management but are under the care of a public school kindergartner during the regular hours for kindergarten classes. In 1926 the budget for kindergartens totalled $2,756,143.

KINDERGARTEN METHODS IN THE FIRST GRADE

Kindergarten extension classes are really first grades taught by kindergarten teachers and carrying some of the methods of the kindergarten into the first grade. Many teachers feel that the change from kindergarten to the regular first grade is often too radical, and that a first grade which carries over some of the kindergarten freedom and utilizes play instincts and interests will allow the children to develop as rapidly and in a healthier and happier way. Children enter kindergarten at five years of age or even at four in schools where there is room to accommodate the younger ones. The admission age for kindergarten extension classes is six years.

Here, too, children are required to fulfill certain standards of health habits, courtesy, responsibility and initiative, in addition to the regular first grade requirements. Kindergarten extension classes are limited to an attendance of forty, with a session of four hours, as are all the first grade classes.

PROBLEMS OF TEACHING AND SUPERVISION

In order to learn the needs of each pupil, a kindergarten teacher tries to know the mothers of her charges. She has from twenty to twenty-five children a session and usually teaches two sessions a day, one in the morning and one in the afternoon, so that her daily quota of children is rarely less than fifty. Two teachers are provided in rooms in which from forty to fifty children are present each session. The kindergarten teacher holds mothers' meetings and visits the children's homes. Something like 35,000 such visits are made annually by kindergarten teachers, and 2,500 mothers' meetings with an attendance of approximately 60,000 are held each year. Mothers' clubs are formed and hold annual conventions.

A special problem of the kindergarten teacher grows out of the fact that children enter and are promoted from kindergarten solely on the basis of age. Consequently children enter at any and all times. Vaccination is another cause of late entrance. Too many parents delay the required vaccination and thereby deprive their children of much of the training the kindergarten offers.

The kindergartens are in charge of a director and two assistant directors. The staff assigned to the supervision of 1,079 classes is of the same size as it was at the time of the consolidation of the five boroughs in the '90's when there were only 89 classes. Each supervisor is now assigned to an average of 360 classes, located in approximately 175 different school buildings. Classroom supervision thus becomes almost an impossible task. In an effort to obviate this difficulty many after-school conferences must be held, and a plan of inter-school visiting for teachers and supervisors has been worked out.

Plans for the Future

Every good department has, of course, its hopes and plans for future development. The kindergartners hope, in the first place, for an increased staff, the better to take care of their 41,000 pupils from homes of many different nationalities and varied stages of culture and knowledge. They plan, of course, for the establishment of kindergarten and kindergarten extension classes in every school where there are enough children to form them. As to buildings and equipment, plans of the Building Department approved by the Superintendent promise that in each new elementary school building the space usually occupied by three classrooms will be divided into two classrooms, twenty-four by forty-two feet, one for kindergarten and one for the kindergarten extension. Each room will contain movable chests for blocks, a work bench, bulletin board, individual locker cupboards, and other equipment necessary to good kindergarten work. These new rooms will meet a very definite need, for lack of floor space has limited the children's activities in many schools.

II. IN THE ELEMENTARY SCHOOLS

IN the elementary schools, including all grades from the kindergarten through the 8B, with their 900,000 pupils, the task of offering each child exactly the amount and kind of training each should have is one to trouble the most farsighted of educators.

THE MAGNITUDE OF THE PROBLEM

How, for example, are teachers going to fit into the same school system Arturo whose parents have just come from Italy, Joseph who is inclined to be "cocky" because he knows English and his parents do not, Mary whose father is a college professor, and Hulda who is thirteen years old and has never attended school?

Assigned to this task are some 23,000 teachers variously equipped by training and native ability. Some have been trained in the new ways, others are so experienced in old ways that change is difficult and perhaps unwise. Guiding the teachers' work are 1,173 principals, teachers-in-charge and assistants to principals, assigned to elementary and junior high schools. It is difficult to separate junior high schools from the regular elementary schools because the junior high school department is often housed in the same building as an elementary school and the lower grades included in the same organization. The principals preside over schools varying in size from 30 pupils in P. S. 27, Richmond, to 4,106 in P. S. 156 Brooklyn. Some principals have many annexes under their jurisdiction in addition to their main school.

Up until a year or so ago there still remained a little one room school—a veritable little red school house where one teacher taught all subjects and nearly all grades.

Considerable responsibility for administering these varied schools rests upon the district superintendent. However, he supervises not only the regular day elementary schools but also the continuation schools, lecture centers, recreation and community centers, and evening schools in his district. The fact that one district superintendent—in districts 26 and 27 Brooklyn—presides over 65,000 pupils and 1,500 teachers suggests the temptation to over-standardize schools. Among his functions are the actual supervision of teachers and principals, and the establishment of standards in school work for his district through the examination of pupils for promotion and graduation.

How the Children Are Graded

One difficulty in the way of establishing standards and at the same time allowing elasticity of program is this: if standards are to be kept high for all schools—a laudable and necessary aim—it is difficult to allow sufficient freedom from generally useful rules and regulations for the experiments necessary to bring about needed changes. To surmount this difficulty the Board of Superintendents have from time to time selected certain schools to undertake experimental work.

Experimental Schools

Operating under the supervision of the Bureau of Reference, Research and Statistics, these schools seek to conduct their experiments in a scientific way, keeping accurate data and comparing the results of various controlled experiments. The plan for research done by the Bureau in these selected schools is that it be concerned with the practical problems which the district superintendents find creeping up in classroom situations, and that it give to the teachers and principals definite facts that will help them in every day work.

The schools are allowed considerable latitude with curriculum and course of study, and, being selected schools, are conducted for the most part by teachers of unusual ability.

The work of the experimental schools is a significant factor in producing scientific change and progress in the school system. These schools have played an important part in the re-classification of pupils according to ability rather than chronological age, and in the preparation of courses of study adapted to the new classifications.

Grading Children by Ability

Taking a rapid and decisive step toward the goal of suiting the school to individual child needs, the Superintendent of Schools three years ago issued a general order that all elementary and junior high schools in the city classify pupils according to their ability to learn. Wherever there are enough children in a grade for three or more classes they are so divided that one class may be for pupils capable of rapid progress, another for normal children, another for the slow. Where there cannot be three classes to a grade there must be two, and in smaller schools where there is only one, the children of that class must be divided accord-

IN ELEMENTARY SCHOOLS

ing to ability into sections, the teacher varying the work so that each section may progress as rapidly or do as much work as possible.

This plan of grading children by ability and not by age and of using scientific tests grew out of the realization on the part of educators that a sense of accomplishment and power to attain success is necessary to make a child happy and energetic in his school work. A child loses heart and grows to hate school when he is always being "left back" and scolded and prodded by teachers and parents—often in an effort to have him do work he is wholly incapable of doing. On the other hand children who slide through school without work because school is easy for them often form habits of laziness or get into mischief simply because they have not enough to do and are bored.

With the order from the Superintendent's office that all pupils in the schools be re-classified according to ability there came no definite instructions as to how this regrading was to be accomplished, the feeling being that each district superintendent and principal could best work out that problem for his own school or schools. As the regrading has worked out, classifications have been determined variously by the use of intelligence and achievement tests, by the teacher's judgment, or by a happy combination of these two.

Intelligence tests to determine ability, or mental tests as they are often termed, have come to be used in many schools. A mental test is a test carefully prepared by psychologists and tried out with thousands of children to establish the standard of mental ability that a normal child should have developed at a certain age. These tests are given to find out what a child is capable of learning; not to discover what he has learned. The ratio between the mental age established by the tests and the child's actual age in years is the I. Q. or Intelligence Quotient. It has been found that an I. Q. of 140 or over represents very superior ability amounting in some cases to genius; from 110 to 140 represents superior ability; from 90 to 110 is considered average or normal ability; from 80 to 90 slightly dull; from 70 to 80 dull; and below 70 mental deficiency. Ordinarily, a child of normal intelligence should be able to finish high school in the regularly allotted time; if he has less than normal intelligence he will probably not be successful in the regular high school courses and had best take some of the special trade or commercial work provided.

Through the findings of intelligence tests, a teacher often discovers that some child who has been backward has the native ability to do much better. She then sets out to find out why he has been slow and to spur him to do the things he is capable of accomplishing. Sometimes a physical examination discovers some defect that may be corrected— difficulty in hearing, perhaps, or some gland condition sapping his vitality. Sometimes conditions at home, which may be helped with the aid of school authorities, are holding the child back; sometimes the child is merely over-timid or is lazy because his interest has never been aroused. At any rate the teacher, knowing by means of scientific testing his capability, puts forth unusual efforts to help him, and often with startling and gratifying results. Often the teacher comes to a better understanding, too, of the difficulties facing a hard-working boy or girl in her class who actually has not the ability to do the work that the others do in the same time.

Achievement tests have been worked out by the psychologists in many of the school subjects, such as spelling, reading, and arithmetic, establishing certain standards of excellence which the child should have attained in a certain grade. These tests, together with the regular examinations in the work covered and the teacher's judgment as to a pupil's ability, are usually deciding factors at the end of the term in grouping pupils for the next term into rapid, normal and slow divisions. Some schools use both intelligence and achievement tests with the teacher making the final decision on the basis of these results. Many schools prefer to rely on the teacher's judgment; many have not properly trained people to administer the tests and so the tests are not given. But their use seems to be steadily increasing and probably in a few years intelligence and achievement tests will be in universal use in New York City schools.

To help in the work of assigning children to the proper groups, the schools have found it necessary to establish a number of special classes where a teacher with a small group of children can give individual help to those who need it. The regular classes range in size from 40 to 45 pupils on the average; special classes from 20 to 30. For many years schools in foreign districts have had special classes, often termed "C" classes, to teach English to foreign children. Most schools that are large enough maintain several opportunity classes, where children who are backward in their work on account of illness, or long absence, or too frequent transfer from school to school or from any cause whatever, may have a chance to make up work and to go ahead faster than they could in a large class. For the exceptionally bright child special rapid advancement classes similarly allow an opportunity to progress faster than the regular grade group so that the child often accomplishes three terms' work in two.

Some Illustrative Cases

Some hypothetical cases will serve to show how this plan works out. Arturo, the Italian immigrant boy, for example, is of average intelligence and quickly learns the language. He enters school in the class for foreigners where a special teacher teaches English first of all and other subjects only incidentally. After a year in the foreign language class, he is given an intelligence test. As a result of the test and of his teacher's judgment he is considered ready for the 5th grade. He is twelve, somewhat over-age because of his language handicap, but capable of going ahead in the 5th grade with normal ten-year-olds or eleven-year-olds in the middle section of his class. The school had already made special preparations to meet Arturo's needs—the class for foreigners—but now that he is in a class with children near his own age and ability he will take the regular work until he reaches junior high school. There, or even earlier if he is lucky enough to go to a pre-vocational school, Arturo may begin preparation for a trade. For Arturo's parents, so newly arrived from Italy, have not much money, nor have they yet accepted the value that Americans set upon education. Arturo will probably have to leave school to go to work as soon as he is old enough—at fourteen if he has been graduated from the 8th grade by then, at fifteen if he has not but has completed 7A, or at sixteen in any case.

Joseph offers a number of special problems. For all that he is sure he knows more than his parents, the intelligence tests show that he is not capable of keeping up with Arturo or any of the normal middle group of children in the 5th grade. He must make progress slowly; without special attention he might very easily make no progress at all. When Joseph had to compete with bright children or even normal children in a miscellaneous group he soon found that he could be successful only in mischief; he became a show-off just to counteract the effect of daily bad marks and reproofs from the teacher. But in a smaller class—the slow pupils are assigned in small classes—where the teacher can give him especial attention, Joseph can feel the thrill of occasionally doing something better than others in his class, and Joseph, as his teacher knows, is a boy to be greatly stimulated thereby.

Mary is inclined to be "cocky" too, but for a different reason from Joseph's. She has always found school so very easy that she could lord it over her classmates and had begun to think Mary a very smart girl. Now she is put into the A or the highest section of her class where she must compete with children of notable ability. She soon finds that it is not so easy to lord it over this group, and that if she wants any distinction at all she must begin to work for it. If she shows great energy and ability in this section, she, with others of her class, may be put into a rapid advancement class and be allowed to take the work of three years in two. She will not skip a whole term of work, as bright children used to be allowed to do, but she will actually take all the essential work of three grades in two. If there are not enough children in the school to make a rapid advancement class for the 5th grade or if Mary is too young to go on to a higher grade her teacher will simply provide the class with additional work—a new subject entirely perhaps, or some special project in geography or history, in handcraft or music. One school allows the highest sections of the lower grades to begin the study of French so that by the time they reach junior high school they can talk it quite well. She will be required to do more reading, to write more compositions. She will be kept so busy that she will not have a chance to be lazy or to feel superior because school is too easy for her.

Now Hulda presents a wholly different problem. Newly arrived from the West Indies, she is starting to school for the first time at thirteen years of age. For a while she will have to go into the opportunity class if the school is large enough to have an opportunity class. If Hulda is intelligent and works hard she may soon be transferred to a regular third or fourth grade where the teacher will let her progress as fast as possible. When she finishes the 5B she may be transferred to a special class in junior high school to take a millinery or dressmaking course and receive a special junior high school certificate. One school, 119 Manhattan, provides a special trade cooking course, allowing over-age girls of the regular elementary school grades to learn marketing, cooking, serving, and cafeteria management in a cafeteria run at the school especially to offer that trade training.

These are only a few scattered cases typical only in that they suggest the variety of problems confronting teachers and administrators in a large New York City school. Farther along in this volume will be discussed the special classes to take care of all handicapped children, including those with mental, physical or social and environmental handicaps. This section treats only of the great mass of children of all ages and abilities whom the schools used to try to teach in miscellaneous groups.

Adjusting Courses of Study

When school children have been re-classified into three groups according to ability the courses of study must be carefully modified to meet the needs of the groups above and below the normal classification. The Bureau of Reference, Research and Statistics is constantly working on these courses and has prepared "The Suggested Course of Study for Dull Normals," adjusting the regular course of study on the basis of results obtained with these children. Teachers in the experimental schools are also working on an adjusted course of study for bright children which will probably give more work in the arts, handcraft, languages, etc., and also more extensive work on the material usually covered in a grade's work.

A very real problem of maintaining standards meets the experimenter who strives to adjust the course of study to children's varied abilities. For example, the modified course of study for the slow pupils includes only certain minimum essentials in the three R's and the geography, civics and history that are the backbone of a course of study. The normal and bright sections of each class take more work and are required to acquire more information. Until a boy or girl in the slow section of the class gets to 8B he is promoted under the new "Suggested Course" at the same time that the other two sections are. Ninety-five percent of the children in the experimental schools are now promoted every year, whereas previously the average promotion was only eighty-five percent. But arriving in the 8B the slow pupil is there required to take the regular work without modification because he must pass the regulation tests for graduation. If he is allowed to graduate with only such minimum requirements as he is able to fulfill, standards are automatically lowered,—or such has been the conception of things in the past. Probably some plan will be worked out for giving to the slow groups special certificates of graduation based on minimum requirements.

What the Children Are Being Taught

Now that it has been seen how teachers and supervisors are trying to make easier and more effective the task of giving each child what he needs by means of teaching children of like ability together and of establishing special rapid advancement classes, classes for foreigners, and opportunity classes, it will be in order next to see what the schools are trying to give them. Up to the fourth grade greatest effort is put upon the business of learning to read and write and spell and it is only beginning with the fourth grade that the special lines of study begin to come in. But from there on the term minimum would seem a most diminutive term to apply to all the branches of knowledge deemed essential. New York schools have no general course of study but rather many syllabi as follows:

English—including Reading, Literature, Word Study and Spelling, Oral and Written Composition and Grammar
Arithmetic
History
Geography
Civics
Penmanship
Music
Sewing and Constructive Work
Cooking
Moral Education
Manners and Conduct
Fire and Accident Prevention
Foreign Accent
Humane Education (required by special state law)
Nature and Environment
Use of Library Books
Hygiene
Physical Education
Science

The following schedule will indicate the time allotted to each per week:

TIME SCHEDULE FOR ELEMENTARY SCHOOLS

	1st Year Minutes		2nd Year Minutes		3rd Year Minutes		4th Year Minutes		5th Year Minutes		6th Year Minutes		7th Year Minutes		8th Year Minutes	
	Min.	Max.	Min.	Max.	Min.	Max.	Min.	Max.	Min.	Max.	Min.	Max.	Min.	Max.	Min.	Max.
Opening Exercises	75	75	75	75	75	75	75	75	75	75	75	75	75	75	75	75
Arithmetic	90	125	180	240	150	240	150	300	150	270	150	240	200	289	200	280
Drawing	90	120	90	120	90	120	90	120	90	120	90	120	80	120	80	120
English	495	705	615	705	615	675	525	555	405	555	405	585	340	420	380	540
Music	60	60	60	60	60	60	60	60	60	60	60	60	60	80	60	80
Nature Study	60	90	60	90	60	90	60	90	..	..	..	..	..	..	..	..
Penmanship	75	75	75	75	75	75	75	75	75	75	75	75	60	60	60	60
Physical Training and Hygiene	200	300	200	200	200	200	200	200	200	200	200	200	200	200	200	200
Sewing or Constructive Work	20	30	20	30	20	30	20	30	20	30	20	30	20	30	20	30
Geography	30	30	30	30	30	60	30	60	30	60	30	60	..	..	..	..
History and Civics	..	..	..	..	..	..	90	120	90	150	90	150	80	120	80	80
Science	..	..	..	..	..	..	..	..	..	..	150	180	120	200	120	200
Shopwork or Cooking	..	..	..	..	..	..	..	..	..	..	..	..	80	120	80	120
													80	80	80	80

In the last two years no period is to exceed 40 minutes and in the other years no period is to exceed 30 minutes. These are to be considered maximum periods.

Provision should be made for certain definite study periods, at least one period each day.

Drawing, constructive work, cord and raffia work are prescribed for boys and girls; shop work for boys alone; sewing and cooking for girls alone. In the third year the girls begin sewing, and the boys continue weaving and basketry. In the seventh year and thereafter girls take advanced sewing instead of science.

The Three R's

There is perhaps no need to justify the three R's, the reading, writing and arithmetic of the school curriculum; but new methods are continually tried in these subjects and old ways discarded. Certain scientific analyses of learning processes and of the drills necessary to effective learning have made teaching more effective than in the little red schoolhouse days. Also much material, which is now deemed unessential, is omitted. This is especially true in arithmetic. Modern schools endeavor to give only practical problems such as the child may sometime meet in every day transactions.

Tryouts of new methods have not always been scientific, certainly, but with the analyses and comparative studies of various methods and devices such as are being carried on now in the experimental schools under exact direction, steady growth may be hoped for in the effectiveness of teaching these timeworn essentials. Thirteen* of the experimental schools have been carrying on for the last three years, under the direction of the Division of Reference, Research and Statistics, a series of experiments in the teaching of vocabulary, silent reading, fundamentals in arithmetic, reasoning in arithmetic and spelling. These experiments were undertaken partly, at least, to meet the need, under the new classification of pupils into rapid, normal, and slow groups, for modified courses of study and methods of teaching.

As a result of experiments, the Division is making and will continue to make recommendations both as to adjusting the content of the course of study to meet new conditions

---

*P. S. 1, 32, 39, Bronx; P. S. 5, 22, 30, 59, 157, 165, Manhattan; P. S. 58, 83, 92, Queens; P. S. 145, Brooklyn.

and also as to teaching methods to be employed in the various groups. For example, the experimental schools, which are giving systematic and vigorous training in acquainting children with the important words of the language find that the children have not only improved in reading ability but their I. Q.'s are higher. Tests show that a large proportion of children, particularly in the lower I. Q. ranges, are sadly lacking in the power to understand and use words.

It may be interesting to indicate briefly what the New York school system proposes to cover in some of the subjects on its list.

History. The plan is to stir children's interest through stories of heroes and great deeds in the lower grades, before beginning the narrative of history in the fifth grade. New York confines history in the elementary grades to American history with important related European history.

Geography. As a formal subject geography begins in the fourth grade with the topography of New York City and a study of the city's occupations. Then comes a general discussion of the form and surface of the earth, leading in succeeding grades to a consideration of the hemispheres and the continents, returning occasionally to detailed studies of the United States, and culminating in the eighth grade with a study of physical geography and a review of political and commercial geography along with the location of places associated with current events.

Civics. Since the war educators have come to regard civics as a most important study. They feel, too, that the most effective method of making children realize their responsibilities to the community is to offer them a chance to participate in school and community activities. So it is that teachers are encouraging their pupils to help in the management of school discipline, recitations, fire drills, opening exercises, clubs, entertainments, excursions, games, playgrounds, class and school libraries, athletic contests and savings banks. The syllabus suggests that in the first three years of school the children "should be exercised in the ways and means of caution and safety, the protection of person and property, and in their duties as useful little citizens." Through the other grades are studied, in turn, the citizen's duties, rights and privileges in the home, the neighborhood, the city, the state and the nation.

Music. The purpose of the music teaching is to train children to sing, to read music fairly well, and to appreciate good music. The music work of the school plays a large part in social and community activities and the school children take part in many community activities. Violin clubs consisting of stringed instruments and pianos are recommended by the director of music for elementary schools. Interest in these small orchestras is encouraged and fostered by after-school violin classes whereby lessons are provided at a nominal fee of twenty-five cents to interested pupils.

Art. Art work in the elementary schools still consists a great deal in painting and drawing, supplemented by a picture study course. A new course of study in art and drawing aims to lead pupils to realize the relationship of art to the city as expressed in its buildings, parks and streets, and to the home, also to dress and manners; to give training which will enable pupils to interpret ideas graphically by means of drawing and color; and last, to equip pupils with a possible means of employing their leisure profitably.

Cooking and Home Making. In the elementary school

emphasis is placed on skill to do the simple household processes, while more detailed and scientific work is given in high schools.

Sewing. The emphasis is on practical problems. Simple stitches and mending in the lower grades lead up to the cutting and making of graduation dresses in the 8B.

Manual Training and Shop Work. Manual training was introduced in New York schools as far back as 1888, along with physical training and acceptance of the fact that schools should train bodies, and correlation of minds and bodies as well as minds themselves.

The schools now have elementary shop work for all boys in the 7th, 8th and 9th years and for those below the 7th grade who are over-age—approximately 95,000 in all. The shop work in the 386 shops scattered through the city schools follows certain standard basic courses, but teachers have been allowed to vary these basic courses by introducing their own special talents and individual interests. For example, teachers who are proficient in one or more of the art crafts such as wood carving, art metal and jewelry or in the application of color are expected to plan their courses of instruction so that their pupils will profit by the special knowledge they are prepared to give. Other teachers interested in furniture design and construction, in designing boat models, aeroplanes, kites, radios and other mechanical devices in which boys are interested make use of these special activities in their courses of instruction.

Pre-vocational shop work is discussed on page 43, under Junior High Schools.

Nature Study and Gardening. New York schools face a big problem when they try to bring to children of the City's crowded tenement districts some of the invaluable lessons of nature. Since the fields and farms that are the proper textbooks of nature study are not at hand, they do what they can to provide opportunities for studying plant and animal life in school gardens, in rooms especially equipped for nature study, and in the parks and museums and zoos.

School gardens afford children an opportunity not only to observe but to do; not only to tell about plants but to plant seeds and watch them grow. Many schools maintain school gardens throughout the year including summer vacation periods, while others keep their gardens only during regular school sessions. In at least 250 schools, gardens can be planted on the school grounds and many of these furnish flowers and vegetables that are used by the pupils.

In a specially equipped nature-room some of the schools keep all sorts of natural specimens which the children and teachers collect. Somewhere in a pan of water and rocks a turtle will be moving slowly about. There may be a rabbit hutch in one corner. In a cabinet will be all sorts of sea shells, starfish and odd pebbles laid out quite properly on white sand. In another cabinet will be butterfly specimens; in another a nicely mounted wild flower collection. Guinea pigs, tortoises, salamanders, fish, mice, turtle doves, pigeons, parrots, even an occasional monkey have found places in a school nature-room with children as their guardians and caretakers.

One or two schools keep profitable beehives. Here and there a school will undertake some special project in studying the ways of living things—a poultry project or a classroom aquarium. Many teachers of the special classes and the ungraded classes have found that their pupils are greatly interested in making nature study collections and in keeping growing plants flourishing in their classrooms.

Thrift

School banks are one of the most practical of modern innovations in schools. In the first place there is back of them the wisdom of thrift; there is character education in the principle of present self-denial for future benefits; there is arithmetic and bookkeeping practice for the pupils who help in keeping the bank accounts.

Since school banks were first established in the city schools in 1916, the total deposits have amounted to $8,453,920.00. And seventy percent of all the money paid out of these banks has been in deposits to 29,464 interest-bearing savings accounts in the city's established banks. Pupils to the number of 135,829 who have begun their savings accounts in the school banks have opened accounts in mutual savings banks—the habit of thrift has apparently been inculcated. School banks now operate in 433 of the city's school organizations.

In most schools the pupils themselves do most of the collecting and recording of moneys collected for the school banks. Most of the city's savings banks coöperate with the schools in encouraging pupils to open accounts. Some banks send a representative to the schools regularly to take such deposits. In the high schools and continuation schools student staffs take care of the school bank work.

Textbooks and Libraries

The approved textbook list in New York City allows the teachers considerable latitude of choice in every subject. Every year in February the Associate Superintendent in charge of textbooks sends out to publishers of school books a circular suggesting that they submit samples of books they wish to have included on the approved textbook list. The Associate Superintendent reviews these samples or has them reviewed and makes recommendations to the Board of Superintendents regarding them. By the end of July the Board of Superintendents will have given its approval to selected books; the list then goes to the Board of Education for final approval. This finally approved list is sent to the Bureau of Supplies, which gets price lists from the publishers and prepares the printed list of textbooks from which teachers and principals are required to select the books they use.

For the use of pupils and teachers the Bureau of Libraries maintains over 10,000 libraries in the school—9,501 grade libraries in elementary schools, 436 teachers' reference libraries, 36 high school and 49 junior high school libraries, and a central library at the Board of Education building.

Specially trained librarians are furnished by the Board for high school libraries. According to a ruling of the Regents, the junior high schools should also have in charge of their libraries teachers with at least one year of library training. The library in junior high schools is often a regular "shop" where the teacher gives library lessons and encourages reading clubs.

Many of the new elementary schools have specially equipped library rooms which are often used as regular classrooms because of crowded conditions in the schools. Grade or class libraries are still maintained at least in the upper grades, although the allowance of approximately four dollars per grade library does not go far in keeping them up to date.

Some Changes During the Last Twenty Years

The schools seem not so different in face of modern advances in psychology and educational philosophy as they should be from the schools of twenty years ago, not because that psychology and philosophy do not work, but because they are too little tried. Yet certain marked changes are notable.

Emphasizing Pupil Initiative

In the first place, there is more freedom of action and of thinking for children in a modern school. Teachers do not generally hold with the old maxim that "children should be seen and not heard," nor is absolute and fearful silence considered a stimulating atmosphere for the well-disciplined classroom. On the contrary, children are often found moving about a room, each quietly going about his or her business, without interference from the teacher unless attracting attention unnecessarily. They conduct recitations, dramatize history and literature, build Indian villages at a sand table, cut and paste pictures to illustrate a geography notebook—working independently, happily, and usefully, fairly free from nervous or impatient tyranny of a teacher. The old repressive atmosphere that makes so many children impatient of school benefits still exists, of course; the scolding teacher, the talking teacher and even the shouting teacher still reign occasionally; but on the whole, principals and teachers are beginning to develop toward children the attitude of collaborators and advisers rather than of autocratic arbiters of destiny and learning.

The feeling is now that children should be allowed to learn for themselves, to initiate activities in the school.

So it is that many schools list in their annual reports on "high spots" all sorts of projects for allowing children to find things out for themselves following that most potent of stimulants—interest. Many teachers use the socialized recitation in which the children themselves organize the lesson with the teacher in the back of the room saying very little and that little only to steer proceedings when they are getting out of bounds.

A number of schools have the Dalton plan and its many modifications—in some schools for upper grades only, in some in the opportunity classes where it is found to be a helpful device. The Dalton plan involves the preparation of contracts by the teacher dividing the work of a term into units of a week's or a month's work. These contracts cover the work—reading, written papers, oral recitations, maps, etc.—that the pupil should do on a certain subject in the given unit of time. With them in hand he may work as fast as he likes, going back and forth from classroom to classroom, or from library to classroom almost at will, reporting progress to the teacher and proceeding to his new week's or month's contract as soon as he has taken the required tests and passed them to her satisfaction. The plan is hardly suitable for lower grades where pupils have not yet developed habits of responsibility and sustained effort, but in the hands of a skillful teacher it has proved an incentive to initiative and rapid progress with pupils above the fifth or sixth grades.

Modernizing Subject Matter

Another marked difference between the schools of today and those of the last generation is the growing content of the course of study. The World War unalterably changed and increased the scope of material to be considered in civics, history, geography, reading. Modern scientific inventions and discoveries and ever more complicated social and economic problems must have their influence on what is taught in schools. The schools must keep up with the times, and rapidly moving times they are.

Utilizing Modern Inventions

Modern science is opening up to educators such vast possibilities—and responsibilities—as to leave them breathless. Moving pictures—what may not be done with them by showing children just what happened in history instead of giving them a story on a printed page? How much more real can geography be made when actual scenes from other lands flash before the pupils on the screen. Nature study, hygiene, civics may be learned from direct observation. The abstractions of the printed page, so difficult for some children, become concrete when this modern device is impressed for service in the teaching profession.

Then comes the radio, with its opportunities for putting children directly in contact with current happenings. They may actually hear the President's inaugural address, or a description of Lieutenant Commander Byrd's momentous flight over the North Pole. Learning becomes not a bore but a truly thrilling adventure.

Now how much have the New York schools so far made use of these two great modern devices? With radio there has been nothing done in an official and organized way, due probably to the present difficulties in the way of controlling radio program sources. A number of schools have been wired so that radio may be installed in every room. Many make considerable use of classroom sets often furnished by parent's associations or other outside agencies.

But with visual instruction, in which motion pictures play a major part, New York City has gone far. Beginning a few years ago with one course in one subject in three or four schools, ten specific courses have now been prepared, reaching with two or more subjects some thirty schools and about 56,000 children. The courses are as follows:

Biology	9th year
Current Events	7th, 8th and 9th years
History	Adjustment classes
Home Economics	7th, 8th and 9th years
Physical Geography	8th year
Physical Training and Hygiene	7th and 8th years
Primary Grades	1st, 2nd and 3rd years
Sample Program	Training schools
United States Geography	7th year
Vocational Guidance	8th and 9th years

The films have been adapted for use all the way from the lower grammar grades to the teacher training schools. Syllabi and courses have been carefully worked out by the Bureau with the coöperation of committees of teachers and of the directors of cooking, nature study, physical training, etc. Such authoritative organizations as the Vocational Service for Juniors, the American Museum of Natural History, the State Bureau of Visual Education, National Health Council, New York Tuberculosis and Health Association, Metropolitan Life Insurance Company, Prudential Life Insurance Company, and the International Dental Hygiene Foundation have given invaluable help.

These films are secured from a great variety of sources. For example, prints of the remarkable historical pictures on U. S. History from Yale University are placed at the disposal of the city schools to a limited extent, and have been effective in making history vivid. The Battle of the Plains of Abraham near Quebec, for example, enacted with careful historical accuracy, becomes a real happening of exciting times instead of merely another group of facts in an unending succession of facts. Wolfe and Montcalm, pictured just as they looked in those stirring times, become real men and real heroes even to the unimaginative child.

Certain teachers in each school have been trained to conduct the courses by prefacing each picture with a short preparatory lesson to emphasize important points and following up those points at the end of the showing by questions and discussion. One or two schools are kept as fully equipped as possible with the latest devices that they may serve as model and demonstration centers.

Visual instruction is, of course, not confined to the use of motion pictures. Lantern slides, stereographs, booklets and charts have long been used to illustrate the work of the geography or nature study class. Invaluable coöperation with the schools on the part of the American Museum of Natural History through the lending of slides and charts has been a great aid in working out courses in biology, science, geography, nature study, etc.

The work of visual instruction has passed the experimental stage, and its infinite possibilities have been sufficiently demonstrated, so that the extension of the service seems inevitable and highly desirable.

Modernizing School Buildings

Perhaps it is unfair to mention the problems of overcrowding and of part-time and double sessions in comparing new schools with old; nevertheless, comparatively recent developments—the cessation of building for school purposes during the war and subsequent failure of the building program to keep up with the growing school population—have made this one of the school's gravest problems. In spite of valiant efforts in the last few years there were still on January 31, 1927, 68,212 children on part-time schedule, 46,998 in the elementary schools and 21,214 in high schools. In addition, 28,924 in elementary schools, 21,310 in high schools, and 1,090 in training schools, were on special schedule, which means that a school is, by shifting of time schedules, made to care for two sets of pupils in one building in one day. Part of the children come earlier than nine in the morning and leave early in the afternoon while others, coming later, leave later. The noon session, too, is extended so that half of the pupils may be at work while the others are free.

With the slight decrease in elementary school population noted in 1926 and with the building program going forward, school authorities expect to reduce gradually this part-time and special schedule program. Meantime, a new type of school has been establishing itself here and there in the school system. These schools operate under a plan for making the greatest possible use of a school plant in a school day by what is known sometimes as the work, study, play plan. In specially equipped buildings groups of children alternate in classrooms, shops and supervised indoor and outdoor playgrounds. While one group is in the shop another uses the classrooms, the third the playgrounds; thus while one group is on the playground or free for lunch the other two groups are making use of both classrooms and shops. The plan allows for the proper variety of scholastic and manual training and recreation and for specialized teaching and equipment, at the same time utilizing all of the school plant all of the school day. The plan has been especially valuable in the junior high schools where the shops already play so large a part in adolescent education.

III. IN THE JUNIOR HIGH SCHOOLS

THE last ten years have seen the establishment of numerous junior high schools throughout the city. A junior high school includes the 7th, 8th and 9th years of schooling and aims to make more gradual the break between elementary and high school work.

THE GENERAL PURPOSE

The establishment of junior high schools is part of the general process of making education suit the needs of every child. Educators have come to realize that children at twelve or thirteen years of age, about the time that most of them are ready for the 7th grade, arrive at a definite new stage in development. They enter upon the period of adolescence, that impressionable age when they are no longer wholly children and are certainly not yet grown-up.

It is a period of bodily change that should be accompanied by a change in the treatment of the child at home and at school. Therefore it has seemed to many educators that the beginning of the 7th grade is a more logical time to make a change in the type of schooling offered than at the end of the 8th year, as has been, and still is the custom in many schools.

THE GROWTH OF JUNIOR HIGH SCHOOLS

As early as 1905 in New York a number of so-called intermediate schools had gathered pupils from surrounding schools into one building to take the work of the 6B grade through 8B, and in 1914 special commercial and pre-vocational courses were being introduced to meet the needs of these adolescent children.

In 1915 three schools, 85 Brooklyn, 69 Manhattan, and the Speyer School connected with Teachers College, Columbia University, were selected as experimental junior high schools which would give to gifted boys in the districts in which they were situated an opportunity to do the work of the 7th, 8th and 9th years in two years. In 1916 seven more junior high schools were added and the opportunity for rapid advancement was extended to girls' and to mixed schools. By 1922, when a survey of junior high schools was made by the Board of Education, forty-three junior high schools had been established, twenty-two of them in Manhattan.

By this time the junior high school had developed from a school which gave opportunity to bright children to take three years' work in two, to a school which includes not only normal children who take three years to do the work of the 7th, 8th and 9th grades, but also all adolescent children of thirteen or over who have finished only the 5B grade.

There are now more than fifty junior high schools with a register of more than 79,000 and three junior–senior high schools. The junior–senior high school, including the three years of junior high and the last three years of high school, was established to take care of graduates of the 9th grade, junior high school, who were not at first welcomed into the sophomore year of high school, although they have by now won their place there and may enter unquestioned.

As the junior high school idea grew, central schools were selected to gather from a number of neighboring schools all children who had completed the 6B grade and including children of thirteen or over who had only completed 5B. The central school was re-organized to take better care of these adolescent children, and teachers who had had experience and success with upper grade children were chosen to man it.

If the building selected was of the regular elementary school type, classrooms had to be turned into woodwork and metalwork shops; a room, somewhwere in the basement, usually, was found for the printing press and linotype machines of the print shop; big tables replaced small ones in the kindergarten room, perhaps, so that junior high school girls might sew and make hats; in another part of the building two classrooms had to be turned into one and typewriters installed. A library and a biology room must be equipped. A gymnasium and auditorium were usually already there. Seats for twelve and fourteen-year-olds everywhere were made to replace the smaller seats of elementary school predecessors. In some cases it seemed best simply to add the junior high school work to the other grades of the elementary school because of the dangers of sending small children to another school farther away; sometimes only the kindergarten, first and second grades were continued in the junior high school building.

When a new building is especially built for junior high schools—there are now nine* beautifully equipped new buildings—these shops and special music, drawing, science, and nature study rooms are carefully provided by the architect, together with suitable gymnasiums and an auditorium. The cost of remaking old buildings into junior high school plants has been slight however. The district superin-

---
*P. S. 24, 40, 64, 97, 136, Manhattan; P. S. 37, Bronx; P. S. 66, 136, 178, Brooklyn.

tendent in charge of junior high schools estimates that the cost of establishing the present junior schools in the elementary buildings averaged $9,000 a school.

What Courses are Offered

The junior high school is really a very "different" type of school from the old 8B school. It offers boys and girls for the first time an opportunity to choose what kind of school work they will take. In neighborhoods where an opportunity for industrial training seems advisable pupils may take one of three courses in junior high school:

The General Course

The General Course leads to either (a) a general or academic high school at the end of three years—for normal progress pupils, or (b) a general high school at the end of two years—rapid advancement course for bright pupils.

The Commercial Course

The Commercial Course leads to either (a) a commercial course in high school at the end of three years—for normal progress pupils, or (b) a commercial course in high school at the end of two years—rapid advancement course, or (c) a job at the end of three years—for those who intend to leave school at the end of junior high school.

The Industrial Course

The Industrial Course leads to either (a) a trade school or industrial high school, or (b) the trade itself—for those who intend to leave school at the end of junior high school.

Even in these courses themselves there is some little room for selection of subjects on the part of pupils. In the general course and in commercial (a) and (b) the children select a foreign language for study—French, German Italian or Spanish. Forty-two percent of junior high school pupils study a foreign language.

OPPORTUNITY TO CHOOSE WORK THAT INTERESTS

The junior high school offers special advantages to three types of children: those who do not want to take the regular academic course leading to high school and college, either because they are not fitted for it or because they cannot afford it; those who are overage and have not yet been able to finish the work of the elementary school; and finally to many bright children who are able to do the work of the three junior high school years in two years.

The opportunity to choose, at the end of 7B usually, one of the three courses meets the need of many adolescent boys and girls. They will like the new work better if it is work of their own choosing; moreover, they have chosen it probably because it is work which they think they can do successfully. This freedom of choice fits in with the plan of the junior high school to allow the pupil more initiative, more participation in school management, more independence and self-reliance.

In the industrial courses, for example, pupils who show ability and marked preference for a certain trade are allowed to follow that trade in their 9th year. Equipment for the shops of the industrial course is gradually being installed in all junior high schools. At first industrial work was given, because of lack of funds, only in neighborhoods where many of the children would leave school almost as soon as they reached the age limit.

These industrial courses have in large measure supplanted pre-vocational elementary schools. Several pre-vocational 8B schools were established in 1915 to give to those children who did not take kindly to book work a chance to try out a number of trades. In the 7th and 8th grades the children in these schools were allowed to take "shops" a half day each day,—woodwork or machine shops for boys; millinery, dressmaking or practical cooking for girls. Pupils would stay ten weeks in one shop then go on to another. Later the time devoted to shop work and related drawing was reduced to two and a quarter hours a day. At the end of their two years they would have had a chance to try out a number of trades and to find out which they liked and could do best. After pre-vocational school they might go to a trade school to specialize in the trade chosen, or they might become apprentices in the trade itself.

But with the growth of junior high schools and the theory that here was the time for a child to make a definite break in his schooling if he so desired, many of these pre-vocational schools have been gradually drawn into the junior high school division, and their shops have been turned over to industrial course pupils. The period of try-out is shortened, eight or ten periods a week being allowed to one type of shop. This shortening allows more time for the cultural subjects still deemed essential to adolescent boys and girls.

A child is allowed to select his trade and follow it intensively in the 9th year. From junior high school he can go either to a trade school or to a technical high school course. The trade schools have not accepted the 9th year junior high school industrial course in lieu of the first year in a two-year trade course, but as the junior high courses are perfected this adjustment may be made.

A wide selection of "shops" or trade courses is offered in the pre-vocational schools and the industrial courses, including the following:

Dressmaking	Electric Wiring	Machine Shop
Millinery	Pottery	Printing
Sheet Metal Work	Sign Painting	Trade Drawing
Woodwork	Book Binding	Art Weaving
Novelty Work	Typing	Home Making

Opportunity for Rapid Advancement

The rapid advancement classes in junior high school have been developed with the idea that in many cases rapid progress will be so encouraging both to child and parent, that a child who may be planning to leave school as soon as he is old enough to get working papers may be allowed to continue high school work. If William Abbott is one of six children in a poor family, that family will be forced to look forward to the earliest possible time when William may go to work and help with the buying of food and paying of rent. But when William's family realize that their boy has unusual ability and is able to take his last three years of school work in two years, they may be induced to make continued sacrifices in order that William may go on to high school or trade school. At any rate William will have a chance at ninth year work that he might never have had otherwise. These rapid advancement classes, too, constitute a valuable economy,—economy of money and teachers' time, of supplies, and more important by far, economy of children's time and energy.

Opportunity to Overcome Retardation

The junior high school is a boon to children in the elementary school who are thirteen or more years old and have been able to complete only the 5B grade. Their tastes have outgrown those of their elementary school classmates because they are older; they are perhaps unable to do the required "book work" although they may have other talents and aptitudes which they have never had a chance to develop. At any rate they are usually not interested in academic work and often cause much trouble because continued failure has made them hate school.

One theory is that if such children are put into shops with boys of their own age or into the model flat with girls of their own age for part of the day, their interest in school may be renewed and stimulated, and their lost self-respect restored.

This theory led to the establishment of adjustment classes in junior high school to give over-age pupils a chance to take up new work which they would like and which might be of more use to them when they were allowed to leave school. In the adjustment classes they are drilled in absolutely essential language and arithmetic skills, and in addition are allowed to select one of the many "shops" of the industrial course. Pupils registered in adjustment classes in 1925–26 numbered around 3,750 pupils. Incidentally retardation in the elementary schools has been reduced by just 3,750 pupils and many a teacher's energies released to the benefit of her normal or bright pupils. Members of the adjustment classes are included in the regular student body, invited to take part in outside activities and auditorium periods, and in short may reap all the social advantages which the junior high school offers. Some schools provide special certificates for those who have finished their trade courses in junior high school.

Opportunity for Social Activities

One of the most important factors in the development of junior high schools is the recognition by educators that a new type of organization and of management is necessary in a school for adolescent boys and girls. They feel that one of the first duties of a junior high school is to provide wholesome means of self-expression to children who are fast developing impulses to adventure, romance and idealism. To take advantage of the fresh enthusiasms and the bubbling energies of these adolescent children, the junior high school superintendent suggested the formation of social and cultural clubs as an extra-curricular activity. The plan was tried and met with unusual success.

At the time of the 1922 survey, 387 clubs of junior high school pupils had been formed in the various schools. The children eagerly remained an hour after school for the French club or the drama club or the folk-dancing club. Indeed, so successful were the clubs that they have now been included as one of the organized school projects and are given a place on the program of every junior high school.

The club answers the need of many children for wholesome social activities; it fosters new friendships, and strengthens new ideals; sometimes it stimulates scholastic progress when backward pupils are encouraged to join a small study club or coaching group to make up a deficient subject, returning to a social club as soon as the deficiency is worked off.

An astonishing variety of activities has grown up in these clubs, mostly on the initiative of the boys and girls themselves. There are music and art clubs, science and literature clubs; sewing clubs, home-making and woodwork clubs; walking and dancing clubs; photography, stamp collecting, and radio clubs. They are all organized and run by pupils themselves, with teachers in the background to advise and help only when help is needed. The drama club prepares a play for presentation with one of their own number coaching; the English club criticizes contributions for the school papers, accepting some, rejecting others; children learn to "talk on their feet," to conduct meetings; the over-timid gain confidence and the over-sure are put in their places.

Perhaps the participation in school management that most of the junior high school principals allow pupils should be considered a social as well as an educational advantage. Sometimes a school is run as a city, sometimes as a little republic with the pupils themselves in office. Sometimes committees of pupils coöperate with the faculty in affairs of school administration. Always pupils are allowed some measure of responsibility in fire drills, opening exercises and changing of periods. Here again, the idea is to allow the children to feel responsibility, to make decisions and plans, to develop self-reliance and qualities of leadership if possible.

Some Junior High School Achievements

Seventy-five percent of junior high school graduates go on to senior high school and maintain themselves well. About 7,790 were graduated in June, 1926, from the 9,423 on register in 9B. High school principals who were at first skeptical of the powers of pupils from the junior high school are now inclined to accept the idea that the junior high school is eventually to take all first year high school pupils, because it has been found that the percentage of failures among junior high school pupils is less in high school subjects than among graduates from the regular elementary schools.

The rapid advancement classes have saved many terms of school without harming the prospects of future progress for the pupils thus advanced. The 1922 survey showed that forty-three percent of the children completing 9B had gained a year from 7A to 9B. Registration in rapid advancement classes in 1925–26 was well over 17,000.

Teachers and principals have reason to believe that the junior high school has succeeded in keeping in school for a year or two at least, and in many cases for a much longer time, many children who would otherwise have left as soon as they were old enough.

Guiding Children into Vocations

Much has been said in talking of the junior high school idea about allowing children an opportunity to choose new paths leading to the practical world where they will probably have to earn a living. Yet few would hold that a twelve or thirteen-year-old child is well enough informed or wise enough to make the best choice without some special information and some special guidance.

The teachers in all junior high schools try, of course, to help pupils in choice of new paths, but their tasks are already so heavy and their time so well filled that they can do little. A junior high school teacher has on an average only three periods a week in which to make records and do all the necessary outside preparation and correcting of papers.

The Vocational Service for Juniors, one of the many outside organizations coöperating with the city schools, has provided several vocational counselors to help children of a junior high school to make a wise selection either of school work or of a trade or profession.

This counselor begins her work with a series of short talks to 7th year pupils about various occupations. She gives them a brief glimpse of the part industry has played in history; she classifies the principal occupations from which they must choose; she discusses the wages, hours, and working conditions of each type; she stresses particularly the qualifications necessary and the training that would best fit the child for a skilled trade, or a licensed or technical profession.

When the time comes for the children to select their special courses she talks to each one separately about what the future probably holds for him. She has information at hand about his I. Q., his school record, his own ideas about what he would like to do. If circumstances seem to be forcing him into a course unsuited to his abilities or tastes the counselor will ask his parents to call to discuss the matter. Usually she can guide both child and parents to a sensible course, but if she cannot the child is given a chance to take what he has chosen. If he fails after one term he is usually ready to follow her guidance, which is based on careful consideration of everything she can find out about him—his home conditions, his health, disposition, capacities as demonstrated in school, etc.

The Board of Education has tentatively taken over the plan of placing vocational counselors in the junior high schools and high schools by allowing $15,000 in its budget and by fixing a salary of $1,900 for such a counselor. There is no provision, however, for periodical advancements and the salary itself offers little inducement to a properly trained person.

The Future of the Junior High Schools

Of course as more and more junior high schools are established those in charge hope to have new buildings provided with all the necessary equipment for allowing pupils a choice of either a general, a commercial or an industrial course. Junior high schools will perhaps never wholly supplant the 8B school because a junior high school plant with its special rooms, its shops and its library, auditorium and gymnasium, will be financially possible only where a district is well enough populated to have a junior high school of some size. But the wide extension of junior high schools in all but the sparsely populated districts is predicted. The instability of the present junior high school teaching force, due to promotions to high schools and trade schools where salaries are higher and "pupil-loads" less, is now a source of considerable worry to the junior high school division. For all except foreign language teachers three years' experience in the upper grades is asked of junior high school teachers in addition to high scholastic requirements. There is no experience requirement for high school teachers.

IV. IN THE HIGH SCHOOLS

ONCE the idea is accepted that in junior high school, when boys and girls have only begun to grow up, opportunities for choosing new paths and for partly guiding their own affairs are necessary to their right development, it is easy to accept the idea that high schools should offer even further opportunities and varieties of experience. By the time most children reach high school they are old enough to be legally free from school obligations, old enough to quit school if they like,—and if their parents like. If then, they may choose, with certain limitations, what work they shall do, it seems logical that if they go to school they should be able to choose, with certain limitations, what studies they shall take.

The Three-fold Opportunities Offered

As in the junior high schools there are three main paths that pupils may take: (1) An academic or general course leading to a normal school or college and such professions as law, medicine and teaching; (2) a commercial course leading possibly to college and a business course, but more likely to business and a job; (3) a trade or technical training leading either to a college technical course and a scientific or engineering profession or to a trade itself. New York City high schools offer varied opportunities along all three of these paths, and, for the benefit of many children whose high school career will probably be cut short because of lack of funds, or of liking for school, or of ability, they offer short one and two-year courses that will prepare directly for a job.

TYPES OF HIGH SCHOOLS

Open to the adolescent boy or girl who wants a high school education—there are now about 136,000 of them in New York—are thirty-eight high schools with forty-five annexes, including: (1) General or academic high schools, usually preparatory to a higher school; (2) "cosmopolitan" high schools which offer all three courses so that children of the district may not have to travel far for the type of education they want; (3) high schools of commerce; (4) technical high schools; (5) textile high school which prepares for participation in the city's chief industry; (6) coöperative high schools which offer pupils a chance to learn from the actual job at the same time they are having theory and practice in school.

The Board of Education has published a pamphlet*, for the information of elementary and junior high school graduates, setting forth in clear and concise form not only what each of the city's thirty-eight high schools and four vocational schools offer, but also just what a student must do in order to prepare for a specific trade or profession. This pamphlet is distributed among elementary and junior high school pupils who plan to go on to high school. Most schools arrange to have a meeting of parents of children in the graduating class at which this information may be given out, so that parents may help their children in making wise choices.

---

*The Public High Schools and Vocational Schools of the City of New York (1926).

Since this pamphlet explains so clearly the specific courses offered in each high school it is necessary here only to suggest, in general, what the high schools have done to accommodate the varying powers and tastes of individual children and to meet rapidly changing social and economic conditions.

Certainly it is no light task to give understanding and expert attention to each individual pupil in the huge cosmopolitan student body—numbering up to 7,000—of a present day large New York City high school. Thomas Jefferson High School in Brooklyn boasted 6,826 pupils in October, 1926, De Witt Clinton 6,010 and New Utrecht in Brooklyn, 6,289. Of course, the task might be easier for Tottenville High School, Richmond, which is much like any small town high school with its 449 pupils; nevertheless, certain difficulties are presented by the problem of maintaining for Tottenville's 449 pupils a four-year general course, and a four-year commercial course so as to allow every individual a chance at work he particularly wants and is fitted for. In the three densely populated boroughs of the city only Haaren High School at 120 West 46th Street, in the midst of Manhattan's uptown business district, numbers under 2,000 pupils.

In many ways the Haaren High School, which was the first to work out a coöperative plan allowing children to go to school and hold a job at the same time, is one of the most interesting high schools in the city. There are now five or six high schools offering opportunities of that kind. Two pupils, usually only in the last two years of their high school course, may alternate on a job, one working one week and the other the next week, and at the same time continue their high school work, completing the Regents' requirements in academic work.

The emphasis in Haaren High School is on the educational benefits to the pupil, rather than on the fact that the money earned on the job allows many a pupil to finish high school who could not otherwise do so. The job is secured only with the approval of the school, and that approval depends upon whether or not it offers the pupil experience that will demonstrate the work the school has set out to give him and that will continually teach him new things. The academic work is, of course, adapted to help the pupil in the business he has chosen.

The Courses Offered

The plan is to make the high schools of the city part of a huge coöperative enterprise organized for the purpose of giving to Sam Smith and Agnes Delehanty just the proper training he or she needs for a useful and happy life. Beginning at the beginning of this plan, there is, first, the diversification of the schools themselves suggested by the types of schools listed above.

There is, second, the diversification of courses, especially in the larger high schools, to meet every need of a highly diversified group of pupils. New subjects have to be added to the curriculum constantly. Textile High School came into being when the war, the breakdown of the old apprentice system, and other conditions of the trade made the men of the textile business suddenly feel the need for trained young workers. Immigration has brought to our shores representatives of almost every race under the sun—and with them certain racial skills and aptitudes which the schools should recognize and foster. Compulsory education laws, made to benefit large numbers of pupils who might otherwise be too hastily forced into industry, have forced into the high school pupils of little aptitude for "book learning" to whom the work of the secondary schools—high or trade schools—presents great difficulties. Old courses must be adapted, new courses fitted to their abilities.

More than 200 subjects or parts of subjects may now be selected by pupils in New York City high schools. In addition to the regular subjects of English, mathematics, science, foreign languages, history and social science, domestic art, domestic science, commercial branches, technical arts, music, fine arts, and physical education, of the general, commercial and technical courses, many special subjects designed for pupils with special needs or specific abilities are found in our high school curricula. Among these may be noted:

Instrument making designed for those boys who are to study dentistry, or surgery, or take up research; naval architecture, including ship designing . . . . Stuyvesant High School
Graphic statistics, machine calculation, machine bookkeeping
                                                            Haaren High School
Dramatic art, stage design . . . . . George Washington High School
Auto repairing . . . . Curtis High School
Journalism . . . . George Washington,
                                                           De Witt Clinton,
                                                           Girls Commercial,
                                                           Bay Ridge and
                                                           Wadleigh High Schools
Short story, Salesmanship . . . . Evander Childs High School
Physics for slow pupils . . . . Erasmus Hall High School
Agriculture . . . . Newtown High School
Problems in democracy . . . . Boys High School
Industrial hygiene, Raw materials of commerce, Commercial art advertising, Foreign trade, Business ethics, Mathematics of investment
                                                           High School of Commerce
Domestic sanitation . . . . Wadleigh High School
The development of good taste . . . . . . Commercial High School

It is interesting to note the aims and methods pursued in some of this vast array of courses.

Art

With the numerous art treasures available in such a city as New York the high schools would be poor, indeed, did they not offer ample opportunities for all pupils to appreciate and understand the various arts, and for the talented few to develop their talents. Under a new plan the study of art is taking on an entirely new aspect.

For many years art teaching meant the teaching of drawing, until most pupils had the idea that art was drawing. It meant training the talented and letting the untalented struggle until they were sure they did not like art and never would. The new plan is based on the realization that appreciation of beauty is possible without the skill to create it, and that appreciation requires the development of taste and judgment rather than of deftness of eye and fingers. The two-year course is to be a course in the principles underlying good art as demonstrated in all manner of things,—furniture, paintings, buildings, textiles, landscapes, etc. The plan is to surround the pupils with as many examples of good art in as many forms as can be made available, in the museums and art galleries and in collections of slides and pictures that can be kept in the classroom; then to apply the principles exemplified in all these other things to some medium of daily life—a dress design for girls, an automobile design for boys. The schools will continue to offer numerous art elective courses both in the fine and applied arts for those whose talents lie in that direction.

Music

Similarly in the field of music, appreciation is the goal. Singing for two of the four years of high school is required.

Talented music students are encouraged to make music a major subject and several high schools offer a special four-year course. Every high school has its orchestra and credit is allowed for this activity. Orchestral work is encouraged by annual scholarships provided by the New York Symphony Society whereby six undergraduate students of each orchestra instrument receive instruction from the Symphony Orchestra group leaders.

Textiles

A word should be given to Textile High School, a school of 3,300 pupils and five buildings given over to preparing pupils for one particular industry. The school was the outgrowth of a demand from the industry itself for trained workers and it is one of the best examples the city affords of coöperation between business and educational leaders to make a school that will be at once practical and cultural. It was organized six years ago with eighty-three pupils and three teachers; it now maintains 128 teachers and occupies an administrative building—the ancient Julia Richman High School—and four annexes several blocks apart. The curriculum covers every part of the textile business—marketing, manufacturing, chemistry and dyeing, applied design, and costume design. There are one or two-year courses for children who plan to stay in school only that long. One of these short courses offers trade sewing and millinery.

Most of the courses offered in the five buildings that make up Textile High School have had to be worked out from the very foundations. For many there were no textbooks, no previously worked out plans to go by. Teachers from the trades themselves were essential and yet these teachers must have fulfilled the requirements of the Board of Examiners—a double preparation hard to find.

Technical Subjects

Brooklyn Technical High School is another new type of high school that may be setting a precedent for the development of other schools of its kind. It offers to boys a generous amount of work in laboratory, drafting room and shops. It gives, in the first two years especially, a knowledge of various industries, allowing the pupil to specialize in the last two years in such courses as architecture, chemistry, electrical science, machine construction and design, structural drawing and surveying.

Commercial Subjects

During the past year a careful study has been made of the commercial courses now being given in the schools. The High School of Commerce is modifying its courses to meet the needs of modern business and during this process of modification has had the benefit of the advice and experience of many of the business leaders of this city. The State Department of Education has practically accepted for state-wide use the new high school syllabi in bookkeeping, economic geography, business law, business arithmetic, stenography, typewriting and elementary business training.

Home-Making

Home-making and home-nursing courses in several schools are designed to meet certain social and economic needs. Since eighty percent of American women are engaged directly or indirectly in home-making, it seems reasonable that the schools which now spend very much more on the other twenty percent might offer to girls who will probably join the eighty percent some practical training for this profession of home-making. A high school course includes usually an intensive study of food and food requirements; instruction in household management, including light and ventilation, furnishing and caring for the home, plumbing, the Sanitary Code, and tenement house laws; a study of public utilities such as markets, milk stations and bakeries; instruction in the art of laundering, including lessons on the different fibres, cotton, linen and silk. Finally, there is the home considered as a social center, as the center of much that is gracious in the lives of everyday folk. This latter consideration has led to the establishment, in many elementary and junior high schools as well as in the high schools themselves, of model flats where girls may practice and demonstrate the arts of home-making with which they are becoming familiar; where they learn to serve dainty meals; to clean and to scrub and to add such home-making touches as stenciled curtains and handmade linens and embroideries. These model flats usually have a nicely equipped kitchen, living-room, bedroom and bath, together with such modern accompaniments as vacuum cleaners and electric irons.

Home-nursing, too, has come to be a regular course in a number of high schools. This course, beginning with the causes of sickness and methods of prevention, goes on to practical demonstrations of the care of babies, and of the sick at home, accompanied always by discussions of fundamental rules of hygiene and sanitation.

Agriculture

It is natural that city-born children seeking novelty might become interested in fields and gardens. It is unnatural that children of foreign folk who have a long farming ancestry be not interested in agriculture, and unfortunate that the great city of New York cannot do more to train them for a vocation which would "come natural" to them.

But only in Newtown High School, Queens, has the novel task of teaching agriculture to city boys been undertaken. There, with approximately 100 pupils, three teachers and need for a fourth, some interesting projects are being carried on, such as: flower garden and poultry, flower production and greenhouse work, landscape and care of grounds, fruit farms, general farms, dairy farms, truck farms, truck and tobacco farms, dairy and fruit farms, dairy and tobacco farms, Indian garden.

Difficulties are many. A year ago the vacant lots, on which the boys had been growing their beans and cabbages, were suddenly taken over by real estate agents and the boys' crops ruthlessly dug up to make room for the foundations of buildings. A plot of land loaned by one of the advisory committee of citizens is now the only available land for practice work. The laboratory and one classroom in which nearly 100 boys and three teachers must do most of their school work is in the cellar of the shop building. There is no greenhouse where two-thirds of the boys who are interested in floriculture and landscape gardening may work through the winter.

However, the Board of Superintendents has recommended that a suitable piece of land be acquired and a suitable garage for farm implements be erected. Reliable farmers have been persuaded to take the more advanced boys for their practice work.

Languages

Courses have been especially adapted to meet special needs of those of other lands who have come to be citizens of America. For example, French and German and occasionally Spanish, where a community's business called for that language, used to be chief among the foreign languages offered by the schools, but now recognizing the city's 803,000 Italian residents, several high schools offer Italian.

GROUPING PUPILS ACCORDING TO ABILITY

The third item in the plan for giving an individual type of education to every pupil is that of grouping pupils according to ability. Not only must the high schools offer a rich and varied course of study that will meet the needs of children from every economic and social class, but they must estimate the ability of the pupils under their care and must somehow assort them so as to group together those who are capable of making progress at nearly the same rate of speed.

Pupils upon their entrance to each high school are classified into three classes—A, B, C. The basis of classification is either: (1) their record in the elementary school, (2) subject tests given by the principal of the high school, (3) intelligence tests, or (4) a combination of any two or more of these methods.

This plan of grouping high school pupils according to their capacities to do varied types of work allows to the slow pupils, for whom academic work is hard, a chance to substitute such subjects as typewriting, shopwork, modified science, extra English or even supervised study periods in place of foreign languages or mathematics. In the classes themselves the idea of allowing all pupils to progress as rapidly as possible has led to the adoption by many teachers of the individual contract, or Dalton plan, which has already been described in the discussion of elementary schools.

Standards are maintained in the high schools by the uniform examinations given in certain prescribed subjects by the State Board of Regents to all high school pupils. In January, 1925, 98,024 Regents' examination papers were written by New York City high school students, of which ninety-five per cent received a passing rating.

Individual Guidance of Students

A high school is organized with the principal at its head and with one or two administrative assistants or assistant principals. Although responsible for all phases of high school work and discipline, the principal and his assistants, in a 4,000-pupil high school, say, which represents a $3,000,000 investment with a pay roll of $600,000, have upon their shoulders so many problems of administration and organization that division of labor demands specialists working with them in other fields—heads of departments responsible for the standards and courses of their departments; grade advisers responsible for steering pupils into the right courses; expert program makers routing 4,000 pupils so that each has everything he needs; and, finally, deans.

A number of high schools appoint deans to take care of special problems that arise among high school pupils, and the High School Principals' Association has asked that deans be appointed in every high school in the city. Deans are at once advisers in school and social matters and officers of discipline. They are experienced teachers whose whole time, attention and interest are given over to students who need help. The dean is a person to whom pupils themselves may go for advice; to whom parents may come to talk over difficulties; and to whom principal and teachers may submit special problems of school discipline and administration.

Many schools have appointed teacher advisers—grade advisers or scholastic advisers they are sometimes called—whose business it is to help all children who seem to be in the wrong courses or wrong groups to find a course or group more suited to their abilities as demonstrated through their scholastic records and such intelligence and achievement tests as they may have been given. When a boy or girl is failing badly and an adjustment seems hard to make, the teacher adviser calls in the child's parents and explains as carefully as possible what she thinks is wrong. Jennie Smith, whose I. Q. is only 84, let us say, has insisted upon taking the full commercial course including Spanish, which is too hard for her. The result—failure in stenography and Spanish, low marks in English, typing, bookkeeping and her other subjects. The teacher adviser thinks she should drop the Spanish and concentrate on English and typing, or else transfer to an industrial course—sewing or millinery. Jennie's parents, ambitious for her, have encouraged her to struggle along with these subjects. The adviser manages after a conference at school over Jennie's school record to persuade them and Jennie, too, that the Spanish must be dropped.

Ministering to the Many Sides of Pupils

Modern high schools with their care for the individual feel that they must minister to the many interests and aptitudes of their pupils. Half-grown boys and girls have many needs—health needs, recreation needs, social needs—which schools can help to meet.

On the health side little in the way of regular and thorough physical examination has so far been provided for high school students except through the Department of Physical Training, only a few of whose men, of course, are physicians. The medical inspectors of the Board of Health have all and more than they can do with the elementary schools, although occasionally they do, by special request, send a doctor to make a series of examinations of high school children. For the most part high school health work is carried on under the physical training department and each child receives an examination of heart and lungs before being assigned to a gym class. The physical training schedule usually includes corrective gym work and hygiene and health lectures. Athletic activities, described in detail elsewhere, are one of the best possible health builders and all students are urged to take part in them.

Hundreds of recreational and social activities are encouraged. Glee clubs, orchestras, dramatic clubs, school papers and magazines are there for the artistically inclined. Dances, concerts and lectures offer evening entertainment. There is hardly a fad, hobby or favorite study for which a club has not been formed. Some high schools boast as many as sixty clubs—more than Heinz' fifty-seven varieties.

IN THE HIGH SCHOOLS

CITIZENSHIP TRAINING AND STUDENT ORGANIZATIONS

Recognizing that training for citizenship is one of the foremost functions of schools, the Board of Education in 1918 made civics one of the required subjects in first year high school for all pupils and assigned a special director to the supervision of civics teaching.

The first step in organizing the course was to get together a committee of teachers to formulate a plan for making the study of civics—or civil government as it used to be called—concrete rather than abstract, participatory rather than merely discoursive. The syllabus in civics which resulted suggests to teachers ways and means of using the wonderful civic laboratory the city itself affords; and of showing the pupil how the government is helping to solve problems immediately touching him and how he may coöperate with the government's agents in dealing with those problems.

When the syllabus was finished there could be found no one textbook to help the teachers in carrying out all its projects. Therefore civics is taught without a textbook. A room is set aside in the Municipal Library for use of civics teachers and pupils, and the city librarians, with the wholehearted coöperation of city officials, have gathered there all available information about the doings of different city departments.

Freedom of access is accorded to children to all city, state and federal bureaus. The Bureau of Weights and Measures will send an automobile loaded with apparatus used in testing scales and in charge of a capable lecturer to any school. Fire houses will stage special demonstrations for a high school class. Bureau heads meet with civics teachers to tell them about their work and to suggest activities for pupils that will make them feel they play a part in government.

Student organizations with school administrative and governmental functions become the practice shops in citizenship. Civics and debating clubs conduct courts and legislature and congressional sessions. Traffic squads and sanitary squads keep order within the schools themselves. Pupils are urged to take part in such activities as the National Oratorical contest, in which a prize for the best ten-minute original oration on the Constitution was won by a pupil of Wadleigh High School last year.

The plan is for pupils to take some of the civics teaching into their homes. Before election day some of the high school freshmen civics pupils conduct effective campaigns to induce citizens to enroll in some political party, attend the primaries, and to vote. Pupils of foreign parents are often able to interest their parents in taking out citizenship papers. One father wrote to the school that his daughter had persuaded him that he should not dodge jury duty when it fell to him.

The influence of citizenship training in the schools becomes even more widespread. It enlists the coöperation of officials and of outside civic organizations and gets them interested in schools.

One of the most valuable of student organizations for putting upon pupils themselves responsibilities such as they will meet later in life is that distinctive feature of New York City high school life known as the G. O. The G. O.'s—General Organizations—are the student body associations of the several high schools. The officials of the G. O. are elected by the students and are most important factors in the school's social life. Membership in the G. O. is voluntary, but practically all of the students join and pay their twenty-five cent dues each term. Funds are administered by elected representatives.

What becomes of the twenty-five cent dues each term? In the first place every athletic team gets its outfit—base-ball, football, soccer, girls' and boys' hockey, girls' and boys' basketball, Lacrosse, track and swimming. Several high schools own their athletic fields which have been purchased by their G.O.'s.

The dramatic society needs to rent a theatre or to hire costumes; the orchestra wants a bass viol, the mandolin club must have copies of the latest jazz, the glee club must be up-to-date and have new music each term; the poster club needs brushes and colors; the French club must have a few new French plays to read and discuss; the chess club wants a new set of men once in a while. All these activities, and many more, are given impetus by the semi-annual membership fee. Besides this, the student receives reduced rates at all entertainments and games.

Of course the twenty-five cent pieces do not do all the work. Some of the games and entertainments are open to the public and are so well attended as to be money makers for the G. O.'s. For example, football usually makes money while baseball is apt to run behind.

Budgets are made at the beginning of each term for each activity of the school. These budgetary requests are submitted to the elected student officials who go over them in true political style, grant hearings and make appropriations to fit the funds.

Teachers and officials of the schools go over all activities of the G. O., but the youngsters are expected to take the responsibility and actually carry out the wishes of the students who have elected them to office.

The total assets of the G. O.'s of the thirty-eight high schools at the present time amount to approximately half a million dollars. Accounts are carefully checked in the office of the superintendent in charge of high schools, audited by the Auditor of the Board of Education and published each six months.

The G. O.'s began in a small way twenty-five years ago. The principals of the schools used to keep the accounts and appropriate the funds. Gradually, as the schools grew in size and more activities were undertaken, the boys and girls were allowed to take more and more responsibility until now they not only administer their G. O.'s but participate in many other activities connected with the running of the schools. The G. O.'s are probably the best practice schools for citizenship and self-government that the high schools can offer.

One of the largest responsibilities undertaken by the G. O.'s is their work in connection with the high school lunch rooms. Seventy percent of the high school lunch rooms are managed by the G. O.'s, the rest by private concessionaires. There is no central supervision for high school lunch rooms although there is usually a faculty member in charge at each school. Supervision by a trained faculty member from the Home-Making Department is highly desirable so that the lunch rooms shall be run according to an educational, not a commercial plan, with the sensible foods displayed before desserts, and the menus properly balanced. Patronage is excellent; the G. O. lunch rooms alone do something like half a million dollars worth of business each term. In one term last year the receipts were $685,000. Salaries are paid to managers and the equipment is usually paid for by lunch room receipts. For training in business management as well as in civic responsibility the lunch room project serves an excellent purpose.

OUTLOOK FOR THE FUTURE

Most hopeful for the future development of the high schools is the spirit of experimentation that is abroad. A rare high school it is whose teachers are not carrying on some sort of experiment, the results of which sooner or later appear in the monthly "Bulletin of High Points" published by the High School Division and distributed among high school teachers,—experiments with intelligence and achievement tests, with Dalton plans and project methods, with courses for the subnormal and courses for the superior, with new and old courses, with character ratings, with programs that make readjustments easy, with school organization, and with absolutely every phase of school life. Such experimentation indicates, of course, a teaching corps possessed of energy, initiative, and a scientific spirit of inquiry that augurs well for the future of the high schools.

V. IN THE VOCATIONAL SCHOOLS

IT is not surprising that with its million children from homes of varied degrees of culture some phases of the educational work in New York City may seem like Topsy to have just grown. A legislature passes a law stipulating that vocational education be provided for children who have completed the grammar grades and are not yet old enough for their working papers. The legislature cannot, of course, pass trained teachers for the work also; neither is the legislature equipped to prescribe detailed courses of study. There are not enough men and women at first who know the trades and who also know the business of education to make the proper plans and specifications. There are no buildings fitted for the necessary work and there is, of course, not enough money to provide them immediately.

What then, can the vocational and continuation schools do but "just grow?" Children are coming to newly established schools from all parts of the city, from many walks of life. Here is a large group of boys who are clever with fingers, probably apt at the mechanics trades. Here is another group of boys, not so clever with their fingers perhaps, but intelligent and intent upon success. One boy's father is in the garment trades, another's brother is an expert sheet metal worker, another has a friend who is making good money as an auto mechanic—and these are the facts that determine the boy's choice of trades most often. The vocational or trade school must provide for each of them the training he needs in the field he selects.

The Four Vocational Schools

In the face of difficult and diversified problems the vocational schools individually and collectively have made great progress. The first public vocational school in New York City, the Vocational School for Boys, was organized in 1909. The Manhattan Trade School for Girls was founded as a private institution in 1901 and taken over by the Board of Education in 1910. The Murray Hill Vocational School was organized in 1914 and the Brooklyn Vocational School in 1915.

Requirements for Admission

Children must have satisfactorily completed the course of study of an elementary school before they can go to trade school or in case they are fourteen years of age and have not yet been graduated from elementary school, they may be admitted provided they pass a written examination given by the vocational school principal in reading, writing and arithmetic. They are not, as is so often supposed, the subnormal or mentally deficient children, although naturally enough there are among them many who like a job better than a lesson and who frankly care little for books and bookish learning.

The Courses Offered

The vocational schools offer a two-year course enabling pupils to acquire an intensive training together with the related and academic subjects in some one of the basic industries. One half of a six hour day is devoted to trade work and the other half to related and academic subjects. At present boys have the choice of one of the following trades:

Architectural Drawing	Book-binding	Clay Modeling
Auto Repair	Mechanical Drawing	Electric Wiring
Forge and Foundry	Machine Shop	Pattern Making
Plumbing	Printing	Sign Painting
Sheet Metal	Woodwork	Garment Design
Dressmaking	Power Machine Operating	Novelty and Pasting
Millinery	Sewing and Embroidery	

RELATION OF THE COURSES TO INDUSTRY

Courses in these trades have grown with the schools. There are few definite and stereotyped texts or courses, which is perhaps best because these of necessity must be changed with the changing conditions of industry. Great responsibility rests upon the teachers in a trade school, for to them is left much of the curriculum making.

Each trade has its carefully equipped shop where the boys work under conditions as nearly approximating those in the trade as the school can manage. Conditions in the old buildings which house the boys' trade schools often do not allow adequate space, neither does the budget always allow for adequate equipment. Teachers keep in as close touch as possible with the trade itself so that their methods be kept up-to-date. They do considerable placement work in some trades although as yet there has been little organized placement and follow-up work done. Teachers of the related subjects, English, mathematics, drawing, science, etc., also keep in touch with the trade itself, and with the trade teachers and work out their courses accordingly. Civics and physical culture are required subjects and the trade schools try to incorporate something of general culture into their work. In the Vocational School for Boys there is a regular library period in which the boys are exposed to good books and encouraged to read them; Murray Hill Vocational School sends groups of boys to the public library to be instructed in the use of its books; Manhattan Trade School has a library which it encourages the girls to use during free periods.

· Trade Training for Girls

Manhattan Trade School is at present the only trade school for girls. It is a most impressive school in a new building distinguishable from the office buildings around it only by its superior appearance. Here 1,100 girls may learn and practice any one of many trades—dressmaking, power machine work, novelty and embroidery, millinery, cooking, tearoom management, laundry, manicuring and hair dressing, etc. They work on the Dalton contract plan so that each girl may go ahead as rapidly as she likes. The course covers two years of work, forty weeks a year, six hours a day.

There is no stated time in which a class graduates but diplomas are given out to all who have completed their work within the year at a special annual exercise. When any girl has completed her course a placement teacher secures her a place, which has been carefully investigated previously, in the trade she has chosen. Her progress in that trade is carefully followed up for a number of years by the school and better opportunities secured for her if she is deserving.

Health receives great emphasis in Manhattan Trade School. Every girl is examined by a physician upon entering and any defects discovered are followed up and corrected. Teachers make much of personal hygiene, insisting that the girls keep their hands, nails and hair in healthy condition. Swimming and athletic clubs offer opportunities for healthful exercise.

Most of the girls have a chance to learn the elementary principles of selling through actual experience in the school salesroom where the products of the trade classes—hats, dresses, coats, novelties—are sold to cover the cost of all supplies in the school. Manhattan Trade School, it should be added, having grown up under the auspices of outside organizations better able to equip it, perhaps, than a public school system, has many features not often found in a public school.

TRADE TRAINING FOR HANDICAPPED CHILDREN

Special classes for cardiopathic cases have been organized in an annex of Manhattan Trade School as an experiment to find out whether or not these children should be segregated from normal children and given separate work in separate classes. A careful study is made of each girl and the training adapted not only to her physical condition but to her ability. Care is also taken to place these girls in positions where the work will not be too difficult for them. Murray Hill Vocational School for boys has a similar annex for boys with cardiopathic troubles in the same Children's Aid Society building at Lexington Avenue and 127th Street.

The special work for the dull normals has also been organized separately as an annex, since only elementary school graduates are admitted to the Manhattan Trade School proper. There are, however, a large number of girls who reach the working age who cannot graduate from elementary school because of low-grade mental ability. Many of them, however, can be trained for certain elementary wage-earning positions where they can earn fairly respectable wages. As most of the work which these girls go into is of a semi-skilled variety, there is no definite length set for the course and no standardized course of study pursued. Each girl is encouraged to remain as long as possible, and when she leaves she is placed at some kind of work which she has shown she is able to do.

Special Problems of Trade Teaching

The greatest difficulty of the vocational schools is in finding properly trained teachers to assume the responsibilities teaching in an almost uncharted course involves. This is the same difficulty that is met in the continuation schools. Men and women from the trades can hardly be expected to work for salaries that are less than the union wages in their trades. Yet, practical experience and a knowledge of the trade itself are essential to the trade teacher.

The children who go to vocational schools are usually much in earnest as, indeed, are the teachers who take double preparation in order to teach them. The pupils volunteer to attend a longer day than high schools or junior high schools require. Attendance is excellent and the trade schools are not subject so much as other schools to the tapering off process when advanced work discourages lackadaisical pupils.

II. GENERAL SERVICES AFFORDED

I. HEALTH AND PHYSICAL EDUCATION

HEALTH and physical education and the care of children's physical welfare call for a program going straight through the school system from kindergarten to high school and training school.

In New York City examinations of children to detect illnesses and physical defects are conducted under the Bureau of Child Hygiene of the Board of Health, as is also the follow-up health work of the school doctors and nurses. The schools, through their physical education department, direct the work of physical education itself and also of educational hygiene and recreation. After-school and evening recreation centers, which also have much to do with health, are under the Division of Extension Activities.

The aim of the school is, of course, to give children the best possible equipment for leading a happy and useful life. Education in the days of the little red schoolhouse was primarily concerned with children's mental equipment and particularly with the information to be had from books. Attention to physical education and to development of children's bodies came later when crowded conditions of city life forced certain facts upon public attention.

THE WORK UNDER THE BOARD OF HEALTH

One of these facts was that crowded conditions, especially in the immigrant sections where rules of sanitation were unknown or neglected, made the dangers of epidemics very real. Thus it was that in 1897, 150 medical inspectors were appointed from the Board of Health to go to the schools and examine, before ten o'clock every morning, children whom the teachers suspected of having contagious diseases. Five years later in 1902, with crowded conditions growing more crowded and a new set of immigrants freshly ignorant of city sanitation coming in, these inspectors were asked to give the whole morning to the work and to examine all children for signs of contagious diseases. They were asked also to visit homes of children absent for more than three days without satisfactory explanation. That year, too, the first staff of municipal school nurses to be employed in this country was set to work by the Department of Health, following an experimental study conducted by the Henry Street Settlement of what a nurse might be able to accomplish in school health work.

Finally, in 1905, people were beginning to realize that to try to teach children who cannot see well, who cannot hear well, who are ill from bad tonsils or poor food or miserable homes, is a waste of time; and that since children are gathered together in schools something might possibly be done about these ills through the schools. The Department of Health decided that the school doctors might examine children to detect uncorrected physical defects and notify parents of their findings; and, the experiment with school nurses having proved highly successful, that the routine inspection to detect contagious diseases might be turned over to them, subject to confirmation of suspicions by the medical inspector, of course.

Alas, however, the notification to parents of their children's defects seemed almost useless; only six percent of the children with defects obtained medical attention.

Thus it was that after three years, in 1908, the Division of Child Hygiene under the Board of Health was organized and an increased staff of school nurses was set to visiting homes to induce parents to have their children given proper care. As a result of this home visiting eighty-three percent of the children with defects had been treated in 1909, as against six percent before the home visits were made.

What the Bureau of Child Hygiene Aims to Do

Now the plan of school medical inspection is as follows:

1. Examination of all children by the school doctors in the first, third, and sixth years of their schooling followed by notification to parents whose children are found in need of attention.
2. Examination of all new entrants to school.
3. Morning inspection by the school nurse of all contagious disease suspects.
4. Coöperation with teachers and principals in Annual Health Day by special examination of children reported as having defects.
5. Recommendation of special cases to sight conservation, cardiac and open air classes and the like; examination of children in the open air classes at the beginning and end of each term.
6. Maintenance of eye clinics and dental clinics for special treatment of school children.
7. Regular treatment by the school nurse of certain eye and skin diseases not serious enough to warrant a child's exclusion from school.
8. Nurse's follow-up of recommendations made by the medical inspector through home visits, making appointments for pupils at hospitals, dispensaries and clinics.

Unfortunately the rapid growth in the population of the schools without a requisite increase in the medical and nursing staff makes the complete fulfillment of this program impossible. There are in the City of New York at the present time, in public and parochial schools, under medical supervision of the Department of Health through its Bureau of Child Hygiene over a million and a quarter pupils. Since January 1, 1918, 185 elementary and fourteen high schools have been opened, providing seatings for 250,000 children in the public schools. During all of these years there has been an increase of from 12,000 to 15,000 children in schools each year. A large number of special classes have been opened including open air, cardiac, crippled and sight conservation classes. As the number of schools and children in them increase, the force of medical inspectors and nurses has been thinned out to cover the area. It is natural, therefore, that not as much work for the children can be done as was done ten years ago.

In 1918 the Bureau of Child Hygiene had eighty-six school doctors and 221 school nurses for a school population of 951,778, giving an average of 11,067 pupils per inspector and 4,586 per nurse. Today, with a force of ninety-eight inspectors and 216 nurses for a school population of 1,118,-185, the average is 11,410 per doctor and 5,176 per nurse. This does not include a large continuation and high school population. There is in some districts one inspector for 19,000 children, one nurse for 6,000 or 7,000 children. And these children are housed, of course, in scattered school buildings so that transportation problems add to already numerous difficulties.

What the Bureau of Child Hygiene does Accomplish

The school doctors last year examined more than 300,000 children, nearly 49,000 of whom were treated in an effort to remedy their deficiencies. Nearly half of the

300,000 had defective teeth, more than 2,000 defective hearing, and 27,150 defective vision. Nasal troubles and tonsil difficulties affected one-third of those examined, while 48,951 were badly nourished.

There is a decided improvement in the general health of children. The percentage of malnutrition among school children is on the decline, the percentage of cases of adenoids and enlarged tonsils found is lower, more and more children have come to wear eyeglasses or have been admitted to sight conservation classes where their eyesight may be preserved. Under the watchful eye of the doctor and nurse, the major contagious diseases as a problem have been practically eliminated from among school children. Several hundred thousand innoculations against diphtheria are made during a year. Vaccination is so thoroughly carried out that practically no case of smallpox ever occurs in a child attending school in this city.

The staff has laid particular emphasis on the importance of giving a complete physical examination to every new child entering school. Any defects found are reported to the parents and every effort made to see that their children are taken either to private physicians or to clinics for suitable treatment. The second examination of children in the third year of school life has been carried out in most boroughs but the huge assignments of the doctors has made it impossible to carry out fully the third examination in the 6th year. The examination of children reported by teachers on the annual Health Day* is conscientiously made. This task has been added in the last few years and has come to be a heavy one.

---

*See page 90.

The Bureau of Child Hygiene maintains ten eye clinics* in various schools throughout the city to which are referred all children who are found to have eye diseases or defective vision and who cannot obtain treatment elsewhere. Seventeen thousand and fifty-nine children were discharged last year after treatment or after having been fitted with glasses. Children who are candidates for the sight conservation classes are examined in special sight conservation clinics where a Board of Health oculist makes the final decision as to whether they shall go into the special class. All conservation class pupils are examined periodically and receive treatments unless a private physician or oculist is handling the case.

A vital part of the health program of the New York Schools is the work of the school dentists and oral hygienists working under the Bureau of Child Hygiene. Their work is work both of prevention and repair. Attention is concentrated upon examination of children in the first three grades whose sixth year molars may be in danger. Many parents and some dentists have been inclined too often to neglect children's teeth, but through watchfulness and care the school dental division has been trying to save the valuable sixth year molars, permanent teeth, for thousands of children.

As soon as the examination is finished the parents are notified if any dental work needs to be done and are asked to sign and return a card saying whether or not they are having the work done. Fourteen operating dentists, eighteen dental hygienists and twenty-one nurses make up the staff of the dental division.

---

*P. S. 21, 30, 64, 65, Manhattan; P. S. 9, Bronx; P. S. 54, 28, Brooklyn; P. S. 81, 70, Queens.

HEALTH EDUCATION

Thousands of children have their teeth cleaned and set in order at the clinics, often maintained by private philanthropic organizations, in various schools throughout the city for children whose parents cannot afford private dentists or who are able to pay only a small fee.

How Parents Coöperate

The coöperation of parents with the school medical division and with principals and teachers is essential, of course, to any effort to keep children healthy and happy. If parents will respond promptly to notices from the school doctors and dentists, if they will have the children's defects treated promptly, if they will attend to the required vaccination of children before attempting to send them to a school, the problems of the nurses and doctors will be half solved. Doctors urge, too, that parents have their children examined by private physicians and given any necessary treatments before entering them in school so that the whole burden will not fall on an already over-burdened staff.

Doctors and nurses make an effort to reach many parents each year through talks in the school assemblies and to after-school meetings of parents and through nurses' home visits. Parents are urged to come to school when their children are being examined so that the school physician may discuss the child's health problems, or at any other time, to talk over problems with the school nurse.

The school nurse looks upon her job as one of preventive education, not only at school but with parents in the home as well. She talks to mothers' meetings, particularly to meetings of kindergarten mothers about the care of their children and their homes. A plan for helping both children and mothers in the whole health education work is that of organizing "Little Mother Leagues" of school girls from eleven to thirteen years old. The nurse gives instruction and demonstrations on the care of babies, which are often transmitted in turn by the "Little Mothers" to the "Big Mothers." Nurses have organized Health Leagues in many schools to stimulate the interest of pupils in health topics.

One of these leagues functioning under the nurse has enrolled 500 girls who hold weekly meetings. The girls conduct their own meetings, arrange their own programs and each autumn plan a huge bazaar for the benefit of the health work in their district. They have been known to raise $1,000 or more in this way to provide milk for children in the special classes—open air and crippled classes—to get eyeglasses for children who cannot afford them, to pay for dental work of needy children, etc. Prizes are offered each year from this fund for the best attendance at Health League meetings and for the best compositions of the year on health topics.

The Work Under the Board of Education

Having reviewed the work done by the Bureau of Child Hygiene of the Board of Health to foster and safeguard children's health, it is important to consider the work which the Board of Education itself does in this connection. All of the health and physical education work of the schools is under the supervision of the Director of Physical Education. This work falls into three distinct divisions, Physical Education, Educational Hygiene, and Recreational Activities.

HEALTH EDUCATION

Physical Education

Physical Education is a well established part of the modern school curriculum. In New York the Welsh Law of 1916 requiring that all children over eight years old have physical training at least twenty minutes a day, has been amended by eliminating the time requirement, but the Regents of the State have fixed certain standards, as follows: (a) Morning hygiene inspection, a few minutes each day; (b) two minute relief drill, four times each day; (c) teaching hygiene, twenty minutes each week; (d) directed recreation and (e) formal gymnastics, 200 minutes per week.

This is a comprehensive program—broad in possibilities and with its status well established, although the supervisory staff should be very much larger.

At present one of the elementary school special teachers supervises 17 schools and 588 teachers,—far too heavy a load. The junior high schools, presenting a new form of school organization, should have special supervision and a specially organized program of hygiene and physical education.

The task of physical education in high school includes a physical examination upon entrance to a gymnasium class and subsequent follow-up in an effort to have defects corrected. The examination given by the physical training director aims to detect remediable defects or illnesses, to detect any organic defects and to adjust school activities to individual health conditions.

One of the assistant directors and two of the thirteen members of the administrative staff of the department are assigned to supervision in handicapped classes. The class teachers under their guidance follow very carefully the schedules of games and exercises outlined for open air classes, for anaemic and tubercular contact cases, for classes for the crippled, the deaf, the blind, for children in sight conservation classes and for children with heart trouble.

The physical training department coöperates with the building department in planning new school buildings so as to offer ample play and physical training space for the boys and girls. Standard specifications for physical training equipment in high schools have been fixed for all new buildings and also for equipment of athletic space allowed to those buildings. The modern high school is equipped for health education with facilities as follows:

1. Two large gymnasiums, locker rooms and shower baths—one for boys and one for girls.
2. Two smaller gymnasiums—one for boys and one for girls.
3. Two corrective training rooms for individual corrective exercises.
4. Two physical examination rooms.
5. Two physical training instructors' offices—for men and women.
6. Two emergency rest rooms for pupils.
7. One medical inspector's office.
8. Swimming pool for boys and for girls, equipped with lockers and showers.
9. Laundry equipment for the care of towels and swimming suits.

Standard specifications for equipment of elementary schools have also been fixed in blue prints available for use of contractors. These specifications deal, of course, with new buildings and grounds. Meantime lack of financial provision allows many old buildings to continue poorly equipped and many playgrounds and athletic fields to remain unimproved. The limitations of inadequate gymnasium space are particularly felt in many junior high schools.

Educational Hygiene

Two assistant directors are assigned to the work of educational hygiene which is the second division of the health education program. Two directors, as a matter of fact, seem to constitute the whole staff of this department, although the special teachers of physical training aid in supervision of direct hygiene measures, such as dental inspection, daily health inspection and the examination and follow-up of Health Day. It is, therefore, rather hard to generalize about the work they do. They can make syllabi for the teachers but they are of course unable to see that the teachers present the work outlined in the syllabi properly or to help them with suggestions and supervision. This check-up must be made by the teachers of physical education.

Nevertheless, much of the health program which they have organized is being carried out in the schools. Daily morning hygienic inspection, one of the most important items of the whole program, is a ceremony religiously adhered to by most teachers. At a signal every child takes position for inspection—teeth bared, head on one side, one hand pushing the hair off the ear, another lifting collar away from the neck. The classroom teacher rapidly makes the rounds reprimanding any lapse from neatness or cleanliness, making pertinent inquiries as to use of toothbrushes and clean handkerchiefs, sending to the nurse any child who seems ill or feverish. Meantime a child "Health Officer" marks the daily records on each child's card.

Annual Health Day inspection is another feature of the health education work which has met with undoubted success. The second week of November is usually set aside for special emphasis on health education, and on Thursday of that week all regular work is stopped until the teacher has had a chance to examine every pupil in her class for signs of defective vision, hearing, teeth, of nasal breathing, malnutrition, or other obvious physical defects. She selects five children whom she considers most in need of attention, and the principal arranges for a follow-up of the cases through the school doctor and nurse. Meantime, of course, the teacher's attention has been emphatically drawn to those children who need special consideration from her— a seat near the front for the near-sighted and partly deaf children, instruction as to dietetics, rest, sleep, and fresh air for children who are underweight and malnourished. School doctors follow up these cases as quickly as they can, making recommendations for treatment or for transfers to special classes.

The educational hygiene directors conduct, with the aid of school dentists and oral hygienists, a campaign to establish among children the habit of an annual visit to the dentist. Notes are sent home to parents stressing the importance of this health habit and special instruction is given the children on the care of their teeth.

The directors coöperate with the Board of Health in its program of testing and immunizing children against diphtheria and scarlet fever. They coöperate with the Department of Health again in the publication of "School Health News." Ten issues of this small magazine are put out every year to keep teachers and parents in touch with school health work.

The two assistant directors of educational hygiene make many physical examinations for other departments. For example, they examine certain cases for the Bureau of Attendance; they have examined approximately 1,200 candidates for the training schools for teachers every year; and they advise the Board of Examiners as to health standards to be demanded of candidates for various positions.

To them, of course, falls the work of making and revising the hygiene syllabi for the elementary and high school teachers. Health films have been constructed and reviewed in coöperation with the Department of Visual Instruction. A series of model lessons covering the elementary school syllabus has been prepared for the guidance of teachers who have ten or fifteen other subjects to teach in the regular course of a school week. Coöperating with a number of outside organizations interested in the schools, they have prepared an excellent course of lectures suitable for elementary, junior high schools, and high schools.

So it is that though the tasks of this particular department are not very definite, and the department not sufficiently manned to spread itself over all the educational hygiene work that must be necessary in so large a city, yet a great deal is done. Individual teachers and principals have taken a special interest in the health education work, carrying on some excellent programs, maintaining lively organizations and doing a great deal of educational hygiene in their own schools.

Recreational Activities

As part of the directed recreation after-school athletic centers are maintained in many schools. These centers are in the hands sometimes of regular teachers working after school, sometimes of teachers from the outside whose names are on the approved list as having passed the Board of Examiners' requirements. Three hundred and fifty men and three hundred women teachers are thus assigned to organize and direct games, drills, and athletics, from three to four or five o'clock in the afternoon. In some schools children may be required to stay the first hour after school once a week, this time to be counted as part of the required 200 minutes a week.

New York City has made extensive use of the part played in stimulating boys and girls to beneficial activity through athletic competitions. The athletic work falls into two distinct parts—the work with girls and the work with boys. It has been thought best not to allow girls to take part in inter-school competitions but to confine their activities to inter-class competitions and annual outdoor fetes.

The boys, on the other hand, with the assistance and guidance of the Public Schools Athletic League, of which the Director of Physical Training is always the secretary, have developed an organization of athletics that holds a unique place in school history.

Back in 1904 or 1905 a number of citizens interested in the problem of getting for public school boys ample opportunities for athletic sports organized the Public Schools Athletic Association and started athletic competition, supervised by competent athletic directors, among school boys. In 1914 the Board of Education officially recognized the Athletic League as a part of the Physical Training Department, and the Director of the Department became the secretary of the P. S. A. L. ex-officio.

With the authority and approval of the Board of Education all public school athletics are under the direction of three committees on games of the P. S. A. L., one for elementary schools, one for junior high and one for high schools. Acting as executive secretaries of these committees are the three inspectors of athletics for boys, paid by the Board of Education and directly responsible to the Director of Physical Training. Representative school officials serve on the three committees; for example, each high school sends a representative teacher to the high school committee on games. These committees have worked out rule books setting high standards of conduct and sportsmanship in the various organized competitions.

Competitions are, with one exception, confined to inter-school and inter-class competitions. Following an old custom the League does send its championship baseball team to Chicago to compete with the champions there; but in general it is felt by the League and school authorities that outside competition will not work for the best interests of all the boys. For the aim of the P. S. A. L. and the whole physical training department is to benefit not a few boys but all the boys of every school. Thus it is that some of the most sought medals and prizes are awarded not to members of winning teams but to boys who have themselves shown the greatest athletic improvement over a certain period, at the same time keeping up in their studies and showing a good record of character.

Nearly 500,000 boys take part annually in the various athletic competitions of the league. The record for 1925-26 is as follows:

	Elem. Schools	Jr. H. S.	H. S.
Class Athletics	127,588	32,628	.....
Athletic Badge Test	14,000	1,100	1,600
Field Days	110,000	80,000	22,000
Track and Field Games	40,000	15,000	10,500
Soccer Football	1,800	650	1,200
Baseball	1,500	600	550
Football (Rugby)	.....	.....	275
Tennis	.....	.....	160
Golf	.....	.....	120
Swimming	7,000	2,100	800
Rifle Shooting	.....	.....	600
Skating and Hockey	.....	.....	450
Basketball	10,350	3,625	350
Total	312,238	135,703	38,605

The average daily attendance in the 163 athletic centers is 35,650 boys—boys whose chief playgrounds would otherwise be the streets of the city.

Of course standards of scholarship and deportment are required of all boys who would compete either in a competition or a badge test; no boy may compete in athletics who has not been examined and his activities approved by a physician.

This business of athletic competition in New York is highly organized; there is perhaps no other city in the world which can equal it. And this in spite of the shortage of proper and convenient play space. Aided by plans worked out with the help and advice of the Physical Training Department, the new schools are provided with adequate gymnasium and play space, but alas! there are not enough new schools even to house the surplus children whom the old schools have to accommodate on part-time or half-time programs.

Some of the United States armories are now rented to the schools and it is hoped that more of them will be open for the use of public school children after school and in the evenings. The parks offer really very little playground space equipped for athletics, and that space can hardly be set aside for use of certain schools or athletic organizations. The League now uses eight large athletic fields in various parts of the city and three smaller ones. In addition some of the high schools have their own athletic fields. The average daily attendance at these fields is 8,500.

In all plans for further development of athletics in the schools this problem of adequate space must come in. So many of the schools themselves have not sufficient play space that additional athletic fields properly equipped for competitions in a broad program of sports are greatly needed.

The activities mentioned above represent only one half of the after-school recreation and athletic activities of this division. The second half comprises the Girls' Branch of the Public Schools Athletic League, which was organized twenty years ago by a number of citizens interested in girls and schools.

The first task of the Branch was an active investigation of the existing athletics for girls in the Public Schools, which brought out the fact that there was very little, owing to the lack of, (1) after-school supervision and instruction, (2) any standard form of athletics for girls, and (3) available space.

The Girls' Branch then set to work to meet two of these needs by providing after-school supervision and instruction, and after careful study and experimentation in coöperation with the Department of Education by establishing some standard forms of athletics for girls, the primary object being to provide the city girl with the vigorous, wholesome, natural recreation and play, of which city life robs her. Pioneer work had to be done in girls' athletics because it was a comparatively new thing for which no standards had been established, no experiments made.

The fundamental policies adopted by the Girls' Branch during the first year and still in force, are as follows:

1. Athletics for all girls in a school.
2. Athletic events in which teams—not individual girls—compete.
3. Athletics within the school and no inter-school competition.
4. Athletics chosen and practiced with regard to their suitability for girls and not merely imitations of boys' athletics.
5. Sport for sport's sake—no gate money.

Instruction classes in folk-dancing and girls' athletics for teachers marked the next step in establishing girls' athletics. They were offered to all teachers who would in return conduct after-school athletic clubs. Two such classes the first year had an enrollment of thirty-eight teachers, who in turn taught 328 children in athletic clubs. In 1925 there was an enrollment of 300 teachers and over 60,000 children were reached by them.

The Girls' Branch was at first entirely a volunteer body, having no official relation to the Board of Education, but in 1909 it was given official authority. The Board now refers to the Girls' Branch for recommendation all matters relating to girls' athletics, and two Inspectors of Athletics for girls are provided on the administrative staff of the Director of Physical Training.

In 1911 swimming was introduced and has proved one of the most valuable and successful of girls' activities. Red Cross life-saving courses followed, and Evander Childs High School was the first public high school in the country to have a corps of girls qualifying as life-savers. It is, however, one of the most expensive sports and the number of pools is entirely inadequate, in spite of the fact that twenty school pools have now been built and are being maintained by the Board of Education. This is a most important item in the athletic equipment of the new schools and the Girls' Branch recommends that the Board of Education will include a pool in the plans for every new school.

Each year a park fete, or rather park fetes are held at which the girls from all the schools in the different boroughs of New York meet on "The Green" for an afternoon of dancing and games. The girls of Manhattan gather from schools on every side in Central Park; to Prospect Park come the girls of Brooklyn and Queens; a park at Sailors' Snug Harbor entertains the children of Richmond; and the girls of the Bronx frolic on the lawn of Fordham University.

A summary of other activities of the Girls' Branch last year is typical of other years:

Two hundred elementary after-school athletic centers and athletic clubs for girls were in operation throughout the city, with over 64,000 girls attending. One hundred and forty-seven after-school athletic clubs for high school girls were conducted with over 15,000 girls registered.

Hockey was introduced as a game for high school girls in 1911 and now the great problem is to provide enough fields on which to play. Last year the League was able to secure the use of thirteen hockey fields and over 2,000 high school girls played each week, but there are many more who want to play.

Twenty-eight basketball clubs in thirteen high schools met each week for practice and at the end of the season played off intra-class games.

Indoor baseball is also being fostered for elementary, junior high and high school girls together with other team games such as volley ball.

Through the voluntary services of teachers, officials, referees, coaches, etc., the Girls' Branch receives $60,000 worth of voluntary service each year; in other words, for every dollar spent ten dollars worth of volunteer service is received.

II. CHARACTER EDUCATION

IT has seemed to educators of late that there is no issue in the whole school program so vital as character education. For great as is the parents' responsibility for molding a child's character, obviously the teacher who has the child in her charge for four or five hours a day must share that responsibility.

Heretofore, although there have been syllabi in moral education and citizenship training there has been no definite "program" throughout the school system. There has been a more or less general feeling that a set program of character education is almost futile—that the character training must be tied up with all school activities; that a teacher must direct the formation of good habits in every part of the day's work. The plan has been to develop certain qualities of character directly through allowing children a share in school affairs, in classroom management, in school government, in management of the school bank and student body organizations.

Through the Regular School Work

Civics in particular offers opportunity for practical character education, and citizenship training through civics as it is now being taught is one of the most effective and constructive activities of the school system. History with its tales of heroes and great deeds furnishes character training by example and inspiration. Physical education and the development of fair play in athletic competition—all these offer opportunity every day to the earnest teacher to guide her young charges in the formation of those more stalwart traits of personality that go to make a strong character.

Teachers have felt that they can fill the minds of their pupils with good precepts and ideas in connection with every subject on the list. Of course good teachers have always recognized the appeal that ideal conceptions can make to children and have utilized children's love of dramatizing themselves and their activities through the forms and insignia of organizations and clubs. And every good teacher of adolescent and pre-adolescent children has capitalized their idealism and their enthusiasm for great deeds and great heroes for the furtherance of inspirational teaching.

Through Student Organizations

In several New York City schools more or less elaborate organizations making use of this child love of drama, of heroes, of ideals, this child capacity for inspiration and enthusiasm, have grown up to be the vehicles of a definite plan of character education. Two of the best known of these plans will serve as examples.

The Knighthood of Youth, well established in a number of schools, is an organization developed by the National Child Welfare Association after long study and experimentation. It begins by interesting children in the romance of ancient chivalry, then brings the ideals of chivalry to bear on modern life. Conscientious performance of daily character training exercises at home and at school will win for the aspiring pupil, one by one, the coveted titles, Esquire, Knight, Knight Banneret and Knight Constant. These daily exercises by which one may win one's spurs embody the ideals of truthfulness, self-control, courtesy, thoroughness and thrift in concrete acts. The child keeps his own chart of performance, for his deeds of courtesy and thoroughness and thrift must be done at home as well as at school. Seventy percent of a certain specified set of exercises faithfully carried on for twelve or more weeks wins the first rank—that of Esquire. A more complicated set of exercises, for a like period, wins the title of Knight, and so on.

Another organization which is being tried out is the Four I League. This is a program of progressive steps by which the child must strive through months and years to attain the coveted recognition and honor for honest effort. The emphasis is on positive qualities, and a definite effort has been made to inculcate in the League certain sturdy qualifications that will appeal especially to boys. The four I's are Integrity—basic and most important—Industry, Initiative and Intelligence. At the end of the child's fourth year his teacher carefully explains the tenets of the League. At the end of the 5A grade, teachers nominate candidates whom they consider worthy of any one of the four I's. A child may take only one step a term and he must be nominated by more than one teacher, or by a majority of departmental teachers, and opposed by none. Each step is designated by the proper insignia and accompanied by the ceremony that children appreciate. The insignia of highest honor is the square pin representing the four I's in a perfect whole. Membership is forfeited for any member whose fellow members vote him at any time unworthy.

Evaluating the Service

But whether through constant effort in the daily round of school life or though constant effort in keeping alive the enthusiasm and interest necessary to make school organizations and their insignia an effective influence in children's lives, the teaching of "character" is an elusive and intangible thing. Its worth may never be exactly measured, nor its results counted. Nor can anyone attribute to this or that teacher any exact measure of success or failure in efforts to rouse and foster and strengthen worthy qualities of character in her many charges. Nor, as a matter of purely administrative efficiency, is there any way of ascertaining how much or how little of effective time and energy teachers devote to this most vital problem of teaching.

These considerations have led to the appointment of a special committee on character education. This committee is part of a larger curriculum revision committee which is striving to readjust the whole curriculum in keeping with modern ideas and practice.

The committee has sought first of all to ascertain how character education is now accomplished in the various schools and to gather data on various devices and organizations, such as the Knighthood of Youth and the Four I League, of which the schools are making use. One of the problems before that committee is, of course, whether or not there is to be a regular character education curriculum—whether or not there is to be a time set aside each day or each week for some sort of special exercises designed to stimulate goodness and to encourage wisdom. It is for the committee to recommend to the schools what it considers the best working plans for the development of character among school children, possibly to suggest experiments, possibly to outline a course of study. It is hoped that the report of this committee will bring about highly effective concerted action on the part of principals and teachers to make character building the school's most vital achievement.

At any rate, the problem of character education is one that is now claiming a paramount share of attention on the part of New York's supervisory staff. The Superintendent holds that although the problems presented by the future of the city are numerous and important, the most vital one of all is "the determination of the character of the citizens of the next generation."

It is a problem demanding, of course, that the men and women responsible for the education of boys and girls be men and women of such character as those boys and girls should possess. It is a problem demanding that standards of the teaching profession be never lowered or loosened.

III. VISITING TEACHERS

ABOUT twenty years ago when educators were beginning in earnest to recognize not only that children must be taught as individuals, but that individuals are the only real concern of any school, a way was sought by which to link home and school together to work for the welfare of individual children. It was reasoned thus reasonably: Of course it is a perfectly impossible task to give children an education based on understanding of their individual needs and problems unless parents and all those directing their school life are aware of influences and conditions occasioning those needs and problems. Moreover, if any one child presents problems to his teacher which cannot be solved in the schoolroom, perhaps some solution can be found through special effort to discover the child's problems both in school and out and to coördinate efforts of school and home and community in his behalf.

Who can find this solution and make this coördination? The class teacher has already too much to do. A teacher, then, who is particularly understanding, and who has added to her classroom experience case work experience necessary for solving social problems in the community and in the school. In other words a "Visiting Teacher."

After several years of demonstration under private auspices, two such specially trained people were appointed by the Board of Education in 1913 to be visiting teachers in New York City. The number has been gradually increased to nineteen, fifteen of whom are assigned to district superintendents, who in turn assign them to schools in their districts. Of these Manhattan has seven, Brooklyn three, Bronx four, Queens one and Richmond as yet has none. The Department of Ungraded Classes has three visiting teachers; the remaining one is assigned to Sight Conservation Classes and Classes for the Blind.

WHAT THE VISITING TEACHER DOES

The visiting teacher makes contacts for the school with parents and becomes acquainted with outside factors in a child's life that may be affecting his success and happiness. Such contacts, needed in any community, are especially necessary in a huge cosmopolitan city like New York. There are a hundred difficulties of crowded city life that must affect both the home and school life of the city children—difficulties that parents and teachers working together may surmount. The pressure of poverty, the close proximity of communities of good repute and of bad, difficulties in the way of wholesome recreation, varying social and ethical standards of people from different lands and different walks of life, are conditions that those in charge of children at home and at school must take into account. All of these things, in addition to just the ordinary perplexities and troubles that a child meets in the process of "growing up," the visiting teacher will investigate when trying to solve the problems of an individual child.

On the other hand, the visiting teacher makes contacts for the parents with the school. She is able to explain many of the more or less complicated regulations that a large school must enforce.

How the Visiting Teacher Works

The first thing a visiting teacher does is to find out all she can about the children referred to her for help. She must find out why John is restless and inattentive and always misbehaving in class; why Bennie never has his home-work prepared although his parents are anxious for his success in school; why Alice seems moody and dreamy and cannot get on with her fellow pupils; why Rebecca with her high I. Q. falls below the attainment of the average girl of her age; and many other "whys" that are puzzling teachers. Her first task is to find out *why* because she aims always to prevent as well as to correct.

How does the visiting teacher go about finding out these things? Take John for example. First she looks into his school record; she finds what his teachers, past and present, think of him, his I. Q., his record of physical condition, his weak and his strong points. Then she gets John to talk about a lot of things—when and what he plays and with whom, when he sleeps and works, what he likes to do and what his parents like him to do. She goes to his home and learns what his parents or those in charge at home have to tell her about him and perhaps about his brothers and sisters and how he gets along with them. Putting all her information together, she has a pretty good chance of finding the cause of John's misbehavior and lack of interest at school. Perhaps he is getting no chance to play at all because he is working after school in his father's shop. He may have to work to help with the family bills; in that case the visiting teacher calls upon one of the many social agencies she knows to give the family some help so that John need not work so long after school and so that he may have needed medical attention. Or the cause may be the attitude of John's parents, who have not realized the unnatural strain they were putting upon a child through such a long working day and are only intent on keeping him out of mischief; the visiting teacher must then change the parents' attitude and convince them that John must have plenty of rest and recreation if he is to keep up in school and grow into a strong, educated man.

Similarly Bennie may have a secret and unwarranted grudge against the teacher; Alice may never have heard of "inferiority" but after failing daily in school perhaps has found a satisfying escape in day-dreams, movies and novels; Rebecca may not be realizing her best possibilities because she is hampered by the emotional strain of her parents' disagreement, quarreling and impending separation.

Whatever the cause, the visiting teacher must do what she can. She must try to show Bennie where he is wrong and to have him substitute a more tolerant attitude for his grudge, if a grudge he has; Alice must be given some opportunity for success—possibly in a trade class or in music or in a monitorship; Rebecca's parents must be educated to the harm their disagreements are doing so that Rebecca's surroundings may be changed. At any rate, the visiting teacher keeps working away until she has found the cause of a child's difficulties and has secured his own and his parents' coöperation with the school in the interests of a happier and more successful childhood.

There are various and complex problems presented to the visiting teacher with as many and as intricate solutions. She is assigned to solve problems of poor scholarship and problems of poor conduct. She will probably find more than one cause for a child's difficulties. He may be tardy and irritable in class because he dislikes his teacher and thinks she hates him. Poor scholarship is the natural consequence. From the point of view of the school one of the most valuable contributions made by the visiting teacher is the help given to children whose school work is falling below standard. In order to give this help she has to do some adjusting with the child himself, encouraging him in the formation of habits of study and concentration; with the teacher by citing to her some of the difficulties of environment or temperament that may be holding the child back; and with the home by showing the parents what homework is expected of their son or daughter, and suggesting how they, too, may help in forming habits of study and concentration.

In helping to solve conduct problems the visiting teacher lightens the class teacher's load and frees her time for her other pupils. At the same time the visiting teacher is accomplishing a definite work in preventing future delinquency. Having first discovered the causes or probable causes of a child's misconduct in school, the visiting teacher must next seek to find the remedies. She invites the coöperation of the teacher and the principal at school, sometimes asking that her charge be put in another grade, possibly assigned to a new teacher, perhaps given more shop work, or a chance in the school orchestra. She suggests to parents ways to remedy home conditions that are in their power to remedy. She herself knows the social agencies of the neighborhood who can and will coöperate helpfully by giving recreational opportunities or by treatment in a medical or psychiatric clinic, or by finding jobs for the unemployed, etc. In extreme cases she may have recourse to the Children's Court to secure certain necessary changes. With the child himself she talks over difficulties understandingly, points out where he may be wrong, and suggests new interests, new uses for his leisure time and a new outlook, perhaps, on his own situation.

A Specimen Day's Work

Perhaps the easiest way to picture the visiting teacher's work is to consider one of her days. Part of each day is spent in school, part in calls at her pupils' homes or at social agencies she may need to enlist in the interest of her charges.

Go to a big school in a congested neighborhood on a day that the visiting teacher has office hours. Her "office" may be only a little cubby-hole down on the ground floor— for the older buildings frequently are too crowded to allow her more space. One by one the children come to her. Tony has been referred to her because suddenly just before graduation his school work has fallen off and his diploma is jeopardized. Tony says that he has been working after school until 10 P. M. because last month his father was put in jail. His mother, too, is working to care for the four younger children. The visiting teacher promises to call at Tony's home that night to see what can be done for him.

Next comes Isabel with her birth certificate asking for a working paper. But she is too young to leave school and has a mind worth educating. The visiting teacher listens to what Isabel says about her financial need and makes a mental note that Isabel may be unhappy in her class and that she will investigate further. Then comes Warren, whose prosperous father thinks play a waste of time, and the roller skates for which his son longs particularly dangerous, because he might fall and break his neck. Warren, who used to take out his grievance on the school, is now one of the visiting teacher's staunchest friends. He is bringing a note from his teacher showing he has "A" in conduct on his latest report card.

While the visiting teacher is talking with him about his relations with his father, voices at the door demand attention, and the visiting teacher looks up to find Stephen's mother and step-father excitedly explaining in broken English that Stephen did not come home at all last night and five dollars also was missing. Stephen, it develops upon investigation, is the family "dumb-bell" and his more successful big brothers and sisters "pick on him"—according to his account—and "lick him plenty but it does no good"—according to their account. Poor Stephen has an I. Q. of less than 100 and hates everybody who finds fault with him. There has been plenty of faultfinding. Consequently, Stephen has formed a habit of staying home as little as possible, of playing on the streets until he thought the rest of his critical family would have gone to bed, and going to school late in the morning hardly fit to do school work which would be hard for him at best. It will take patience and several visits to get these parents and the older brothers to see that the brothers must leave all control of Stephen in their parents' hands; and that the parents themselves must change their attitude toward Stephen because "lickings" can't help his school work, although freedom from fear of his family elders may.

Others come with still other troubles filling the time full. Before leaving the school for her visiting work the visiting teacher interviews Isabel's teacher to confirm her suspicions of Isabel's discontent because of a reproof; then she hastens to call at the Prison Association to get help for Tony's family, and on Tony's mother to get her to coöperate with the Association for the sake of Tony's graduation; then on to other home visits, including a re-visit to Warren's father to see what Warren's good report will do to soften his heart toward boyhood.

Future Development of the Work

Every adjustment that the visiting teacher makes is looking to the future. By providing normal conditions instead of abnormal, by giving a child understanding and encouragement, and helping him to find normal interests and activities she is putting a future citizen, who may have strayed, back on the path to an orderly and normal life.

In view, then, of the lasting good that visiting teachers accomplish for the "problem child," the future of the visiting teacher work in New York City is of considerable interest. Principals and district superintendents feel that the visiting teacher service should be extended to all parts of the city. About 55 schools are now served by 15 visiting teachers. This means not only that these visiting teachers are overloaded with cases but that more than 600 schools have no visiting teacher service at all,—a service that is needed in all sections and among all classes. Children may be misunderstood among rich and poor, by educated or uneducated parents, by the schools in one section as well as in another. A resolution of the New York Principals' Association commending the visiting teachers' work and requesting an increase in the number of visiting teachers was endorsed by 400 principals. The district superintendents have repeatedly taken a similar stand. They feel that the service is not an expense but an economy, that the visiting teacher saves many times her cost. They feel that she plays a large part in promoting better scholarship and behavior, better citizenship, and correspondingly in decreasing retardation, delinquency and undesirable citizenship.

IV. SCHOOL LUNCHES

ONE of the most helpful welfare measures undertaken by schools is that of providing wholesome lunches at small expense for children who live too far from school to go home for lunch or for children whose mothers work and are unable to look after them at noon. This measure is even more necessary in New York than in a small community because of the traffic difficulties which make it unsafe for children to be abroad more than is absolutely necessary.

Lunch Rooms Under School Supervision

As is true of many innovations in the schools, lunches were first provided by outside agencies. But in 1919 the Board of Education opened a lunch service under its own direction and appointed a school lunch manager. This service now reaches 6,000 or 7,000 children a day in thirty elementary schools of Manhattan, Brooklyn and the Bronx, most of which are served from two central kitchens. Food prepared in the central kitchens, with all the economies of quantity buying, quantity preparation and centralized supervision, is distributed by truck to the schools.

Here are some typical orders in preparing these luncheons for one day:

    250 pounds of baked beans
    240 gallons of soup
    200 loaves of bread
    1500 quarts of milk
    3500 portions of pudding
    4000 portions of vegetable or spaghetti

It is possible through this service for a child to secure a proper lunch for less than ten cents. One of the advantages emphasized for the lunch service is that through it children can often be instructed in better eating habits than their eyes and sweet teeth might dictate for them. Therefore no child is allowed to buy more than two cents worth of candy. The cooking department with its trained staff helps on menus and recipes and the cooking teacher usually oversees the serving of lunch and gently persuades small Anne or large Billy that a bowl of soup and one piece of cake is better than two pieces of cake.

Lunch Rooms Under Private Management

Thirty-eight schools have separate lunch services under private management and still ten other lunch rooms are run by teachers or by unofficial agencies. In these schools, of course, a profit is made which goes to the concessionaires. The result of the varied types of management is a variation from school to school in the prices charged for the same food—one cent for a glass of milk in one school, five cents in another, for example.

A Plan for Future Development

The school authorities have been considering for some time plans for bringing all the lunch rooms under the supervision of the Board of Education, and for re-organizing the lunch room management to the end that the cost to the city might be reduced. The Board of Superintendents have made the following recommendations which have been accepted by the Board of Education:

1. That the director of home-making be put in full charge and made responsible for school lunches.

2. That a business assistant be appointed to buy supplies, keep records or accounts of transportation and business details for elementary and junior high schools.

3. That no further concessionaire services be allowed.

4. That present concessionaires be discontinued as soon as possible.

5. That all changes in menus, prices, and employment of non-permanent labor be made by the assistant director subject to approval by the home-making director and the associate superintendent in charge.

6. That two teachers of domestic science be assigned to the office of the assistant director of home-making to aid in the school lunch work.

III. SPECIAL SERVICES AFFORDED

I. CLASSES FOR PHYSICALLY HANDICAPPED CHILDREN

FEW citizens realize the difficult tasks that confront educators in a city as large as New York before they can take up the business of education with any prospect of satisfying results. For, as a sort of prelude to actual school work, as a matter of essential preparation, there are a hundred problems of health and social service that must be struggled with.

THE MAGNITUDE OF THE PROBLEM

Among more than 1,000,000 children the schools will enroll next year, an appreciable percentage will be physically unfit to take the school work outlined for a normal child. There are the crippled children, the blind and the deaf, the partially blind and deaf, the tubercular, the undernourished, the cardiac cases. In addition, there are the mentally defective, the subnormals, the abnormals, the neurotic, the children of unstable temperaments. There are children whose homes totally unfit them for giving attention to school work. There are children whom poverty shadows and frightens. There are children bedridden; others held in detention homes, perhaps through no fault of their own. All children, however, and therefore in the province of the educators.

THE GENERAL PLAN OF THE WORK

Obviously, it would be folly to try to teach these children until they have received physical and mental examinations, until recommendations have been made for conserving the powers left them, and for developing those powers to compensate for powers they lack. In this necessary preliminary diagnostic work New York City has done some wonderful things; some wonderful things, too, in the education of handicapped children in special classes.

The whole plan of the school's service to handicapped children is so to educate them as to offset their handicaps and allow them to live as nearly natural and independent lives as is possible. For this reason many educators have thought it best when possible not to segregate them in separate schools but to maintain classes for them in the regular schools so that they may have the association of normal children and may feel that they are accomplishing the same work. Emphasis is laid upon the fact that these special classes try to accomplish the regular work of the regular grades. Upon graduation from elementary school the children are prepared to continue their school work in high schools or vocational schools. Many go into secretarial courses, commercial courses and library work.

Many, of course, may need to have a job when they are old enough to leave school. It has been part of the aim of teaching in the classes themselves to provide the children with some means of earning a livelihood when they shall have finished school and wish to continue normal associations. Therefore, industrial handwork, especially in the upper grades, is provided in addition to the regular work.

Industrial trade work in classes for handicapped children is under the direction of a special inspector who has worked out courses adapted to the varying abilities of the children and designed to give them training that may later provide them with a job and the feeling of independence that is important to the self-respect of a normal human being. The inspector studies the trades themselves and brings back to her teachers through after-school teacher training classes technical information as to new methods and devices. The industrial work is designed to give basic skill with fingers, needle, shuttle, and does not necessitate expensive equipment. It consists of basketry, rug weaving, novelty making, sewing, hand leather work, millinery, and the like.

Teachers of handicapped children work under a special license which requires that they know something of the nature of the children's handicaps, something of the care that various types of handicap must have, of the exercises that should and may be given and of the handwork that these children may undertake. Afternoon and evening courses to teachers who would qualify for the special licenses and to teachers already licensed who wish to keep up with developments in trade handwork are given by the inspector in charge.

Placement of handicapped children in jobs when they leave school also is under the direction of this department and, with the help of one assistant-at-large, what placement work is done she or the class teachers themselves must do. It is, of course, vitally important that these children go into work that they can do well, and that will in no way endanger their health. As a precursor of placement work itself employers must first be persuaded to give these unfortunate children a chance. Many employers feel that employment of handicapped children involves a responsibility that they do not wish to undertake; and, probably, they under-estimate the ability of the children to keep up with normal workers.

Physical handicaps are the most obvious and the most numerous. The lame, the halt and the blind we have always with us. Since care of the health of the children must be the first and paramount consideration, the Board of Education has placed an assistant director of the Physical Training Department, who is also a physician, in charge of the supervision and administration of special classes for the crippled, cardiopathic, undernourished, pre-tuberculous, tuberculous, and for malnutrites and doubly handicapped children in schools, hospitals, institutions and in private homes.

SPECIAL FEATURES OF THE WORK

The Board of Education has had to make many special provisions for these handicapped children. Auto buses under the supervision of careful attendants take children, who could not otherwise attend, to and from school. Classes for the crippled and cardiopathic children must be on the ground floor, near to exits and playgrounds. The rooms are equipped with special furniture, adjustable in the case of the crippled to accommodate unwieldy casts and braces, and movable so that space for games and exercises may be easily provided. There are cots for rest periods and in most of the special classes milk and usually hot lunches are served.

For all the handicapped classes specialized physical training is required and supervised by two special teachers of the Physical Training Department. Health is emphasized in these classes above all else. Courses that will be within the children's powers and that will yet give them the exercise essential to their development have been carefully prepared for the various types of handicapped children to be given in the regular physical training periods. Teachers are instructed in certain games and competitions that will interest their small charges and at the same time be safe for them. Balls and beanbags in passing and throwing contests exercise bodies and lungs. It is amazing how very active the crippled and blind children often are, and keen indeed is the competition,—keener still the children's enjoyment.

Special classes for handicapped children are limited to a register of twenty-five, but when this register includes pupils doing work in as many as eight different terms the teacher has to work fast in order to get through all her school work, observe scrupulously rest and recreation periods, serve the morning milk, conduct the physical training and game periods and yet devote several hours a week to industrial handwork. Moreover, the buses will bring part of her charges at 8:30, others at 9, take some home at 2:30 and others at 3.

Great care is taken that the education of the handicapped children continue uninterrupted. Clinics for treatment of school children have been arranged for afternoons after school, and on Saturday mornings. When a crippled child is sent to a hospital for an operation, he is transferred to the class of cripples there. In case his convalescent care covers a period of thirty days or more, he will be admitted to one of the classes of cripples in the convalescent home, or a home teacher will be assigned. As a result, the age of graduation of crippled children in special classes in elementary schools has been reduced from seventeen or eighteen years to fourteen, and in some instances to thirteen and a half years. Teachers in the upper grades often make use of the Dalton Plan so that individual progress may not have to wait on the short recitation periods for which the teacher has time.

Classes for handicapped children under Board of Education teachers are conducted in many institutions as annexes of the regular schools. Exemplifying this arrangement is P. S. 192, Manhattan, located in the Hebrew Orphanage at Amsterdam Avenue and 137th Street and with fourteen annexes scattered from there to Peekskill and Pelham. The New York Orthopedic Hospital for crippled children and the Martine Farm for children with cardiac troubles, White Plains; the Blythedale Home for Crippled Children and the House of Mercy for Delinquent Girls, Valhalla; Surprise Lake Camp for Undernourished Boys, Cold-Spring-on-Hudson; Jewish Protectory, Hawthorne; and Josephine Home for Children Suffering from Malnutrition, Peekskill, are among the fourteen. Although outside the area of greater New York, these are nevertheless New York City children and New York's Board of Education has gallantly responded to requests from the various institutions for teachers and school supplies.

The principal in charge of a school like P. S. 192 has what would seem to be an almost impossible task. He must approve the course of study and oversee the school work of teachers in fourteen annexes miles apart, whose pupils present very special problems of discipline or of health or of scholastic ability. Trained teachers who are capable of undertaking the responsibilities and who are willing to live, as is sometimes necessary, in isolated institutions, are not easy to find.

The fourteen annexes of P. S. 192 by no means represent all of the institutions where teachers and school supplies are sent by the Board of Education to children who are bedridden or separated from home and family and schools in hospitals and institutions. Hospitals and convalescent homes in various parts of the city have their classes for crippled and sick children; teachers are sent to orphanages—the Dobbs Ferry Orphanage is an annex of P. S. 165, as is the Hebrew Sheltering and Guardian Society of Pleasantville. Home teachers are provided for children whom it is impossible to send to the classes for crippled children in the regular schools. Indeed, it is difficult here to do more than to indicate the far-flung activities of the New York school system in caring for handicapped and helpless children.

At the New York Orthopedic Hospital, for example, there are six classes for crippled children. One teacher spends her entire time teaching at the bedside of children who are unable to attend classes. A kindergarten of twenty-five or more limping but radiant babies is a sight to stir the heart and convince one that any joy that books or teachers can bring to these handicapped children must be theirs. On through the eighth grade, two or three classes to a room, a valiant corps of teachers is striving to give their beloved charges the essentials of a normal life so that no child shall be without the equipment education offers if one day a normal life becomes possible for him.

Special Care for the Crippled

In 1916–17 the city experienced a scourge of infantile paralysis that left in its wake a sad procession of little ones stumbling their way into our schools. In 1918–19 there were thirty-nine classes of crippled children organized and that number more than doubled in the next four years.

There are still in the schools 1,921 crippled children in public school classes, 1,983 in institutional classes, and 104 who are transported to high school classes, in addition to more than 300 who are receiving school instruction at home because none of the transportation and guide systems the schools provide make it possible for them to attend.

There are two central schools for crippled children, P. S. 75, Manhattan, and its annex in the Children's Aid building on East 88th Street, maintained by outside philanthropic organizations. The Board of Education provides these schools with teachers, classroom equipment and supplies for elementary school instruction and specialized physical training, and also conducts the after-school centers for crippled children. The Lehman Foundation maintains a commercial shop in connection with P. S. 75 which provides many of the school's graduates with jobs where their health will be carefully protected and their lives made as agreeable as possible. The building itself is admirably equipped with baths, rest rooms and an infirmary; doctors, nurses and clinical attention are provided free to children in its charge.

These are special schools, however. It is, as has already been pointed out, the general policy of the Board of Education to maintain the classes for handicapped children in the regular public schools where the children will associate with normal children.

Like the teacher of bedside classes is the teacher of the home-bound cripples who personally takes the school to children who can not come to the school. The Board now provides sixty-seven of these teachers—not nearly enough to minister to all of the city's children whose crippled bodies will not allow them to venture far from home and bed.

Thirty-five more home teachers were requested in the 1927 budget. The plan is that each child of elementary school age receive one and a half hours of instruction three times a week. Specialized instruction for older children and graduates of the elementary school course is also provided to enable home-bound children to become self-supporting.

The work is one of the most appealing that the schools undertake. The home teacher brings new interest and joy to the homes of her crippled charges. The children often make wonderful progress because of their keen interest and devotion to their work. They learn to read and the joys of the printed page are opened to them. When necessary, medical and nursing care is secured through various agencies coöperating with the schools. Many improve enough under such treatment to be allowed to attend regular schools.

All children in special classes for physically handicapped children are under medical and nursing supervision through coöperation between the schools and specialists in charge of the care of each child whether as a private patient or in hospitals and clinics.

Special Care for the Cardiacs

The children with heart trouble were the last to receive special care in school. To avoid stair climbing for them, to take them away from the temptation to overdo when competing with other children, to give their health special attention, special classes for children with cardiac troubles have been organized. There are now 855 such pupils in the elementary schools, and in trade and high schools.

The first event of the day in the cardiac class is the taking of temperature and respiration. In the middle of the morning there is a recess period when milk is served; a forty minute period each afternoon directly after lunch is observed as a rest period; from three to four, if the children want to stay, there is a recreation period supervised either by the classroom teacher or by a qualified supervisor furnished by the Physical Training Department.

Open Air Classes

The children with tuberculosis—648 of them in New York schools—present some difficult problems. More than forty are taught in hospital classes. The Board of Education has secured space for outdoor classes for tuberculous children and children who have been in contact with tuberculosis on boats, piers, in parks and on roofs of hospitals.

For example, at the foot of 112th Street on the East River in the large upper floor of a two-story pier extending out over the water are eight classes of elementary school children. When the sun is out it streams graciously through windows that make up most of the wall on three sides of the building. The windows are kept open as much as possible and teachers and pupils bundle up in coats, furs and hoods when necessary.

Open air classes for approximately 3,700 children on roofs and in open-window classes in the schools themselves are no longer a novelty. To these classes are admitted anæmic and undernourished children who need special attention paid to their diet, to their rest periods and to the air that they breathe. The rest and milk program is similar to that of the cardiac classes. When the time comes for rest period there is a cot drill to see how quickly and efficiently school work seats may be pushed against the wall and folding cots, which have been stored somewhere behind a screen, may be unfolded and lined up in military rows.

Charts of weights and measures are scrupulously kept, recording each child's health progress. The children themselves keep health cards and learn a great deal about what care can do for sick bodies. They are taught to form proper health habits in order that they will know how to maintain the beneficial results obtained while in special classes after they are transferred to regular classes.

Speech Improvement Classes

Under the direction of an acting director and twenty-six supervising teachers, classes for children with speech defects and faulty accents are maintained in as many schools as this service can reach. The function of the director and the supervising teachers is three-fold. They have, first, to examine all children reported by teachers as needing the special speech improvement work. Second, they give individual and group drills and exercises for loosening of tight muscles and for gaining control of recalcitrant tongues and palates. Lastly, they instruct class teachers in proper methods of speech improvement, so that the few minutes of work they are able to give in a special class once or twice a week may be followed up.

When the special teacher arrives at the school the children who need her attention have been scheduled so as to leave their regular classes in a period that they can miss without delaying their regular work too much. They come to her all through the day in some corner of the school building where she can spread her charts and keep her mirrors for distribution. The children are taught to practice before mirrors so that they can see when lips and tongue are not obeying their commands. Special drills on difficult sounds and combinations of sounds are run through, then each individual child receives a separate drill on his particular difficulty before returning to his regular class. This work is carried on through elementary school and into some of the high schools. Many children are cured of embarrassing and detrimental stammerings and stutterings and lispings.

The problem of foreign accents is one that occurs with great frequency in this cosmopolitan city, of course, and here again the Department of Speech Improvement does good work. With prospective teachers, too, who must pass an oral English test for pronunciation and control of voice, the Department helps. A clinic has been established at the Brooklyn Training School for Teachers where the pupil-teachers may have help in overcoming any slight speech defects that endanger their teaching licenses.

The School for the Deaf

One of the most difficult problems is the education of the wholly or partially deaf. Even if there were room in public institutions, parents hesitate to send such children to them. Many have not money to send their afflicted boys and girls to private schools. Back in 1908, therefore, at the special request of a group of parents who could not afford special teaching for their children, the Board of Education undertook, experimentally, the education of the deaf in a special school. They took an old building at first, because they were merely to try out the plan. The first year there were forty-seven pupils; last year there were more than 400 in a new building on East 24th Street.

The children are examined first by the medical inspector in their own school. Then cases recommended for the School for the Deaf are sent to the clinic maintained there with outside help for the examination and treatment of children who cannot afford treatment elsewhere.

Only the children who cannot get along in the regular schools are admitted to this school. Sometimes children who have failed two or three times in 1A and 2A grades are found upon examination to have failed simply because they did not hear well. This fact emphasizes the conviction of every person who has to do with the administration of economical and preventive measures in health and educational work—the examination should come before the child has been allowed to fail two or three times because of his physical handicap. Failure has discouraged him and several terms have been wasted both for the school and for the child. Physical and mental examination of children before entering or in their first term of school—that is the goal toward which serious-minded educators are looking.

The teachers are carefully trained to the very special kind of teaching they have undertaken. They serve a year of apprenticeship in the school, observing and practicing as a part of their training.

It is perhaps unnecessary to go into the infinite demands on patience that this teaching makes, but the major difficulty might be suggested. The totally deaf child has no language, no medium of communication except by touch and gesture. The teacher must build up for him letter by letter, syllable by syllable, not only the ability to read sounds from the lips and throat of the speaker, but she also must teach him to reproduce vocally that which he can understand although he has never heard it. The problem of the partially deaf is somewhat easier but they too must read from lips, must be carefully trained in the reproduction of sounds that they have heard only imperfectly.

As one goes from a class where the children have been in school only one term to an 8B class it is thrilling to note the progress accomplished. In the 1B eager little children hop, skip, jump, walk, run, at a monosyllabic command read from the teacher's lips; they point out the picture of a boy, a doll, or a wagon, in response to a noun pronounced by the teacher; they recognize and reproduce in varying stages of imperfection the sounds, b, r, oy, an, etc. Next they begin to put these sounds together and identify them with objects or acts.

In the 8B grade the children are able to read quickly from the speaker's lips, and to talk interestingly and intelligently in reply. These children do the work of all the grades in only a little more time than is allotted the regular schools. They are allowed six years to do the work of the first difficult three years of "learning the language" and from then on keep up with the regular classes.

Teachers in the School for the Deaf are continually experimenting with teaching methods. No one knows what the best methods are. They try rhythm work, they experiment with vibrations in an attempt to establish somehow a standard of pitch for the voices of these children who have never heard. A vocal music course is now being tried out under the supervision of the Director of Music and one of his assistants, to stimulate what measure of hearing the children may retain and to help them with tone and rhythm.

SPECIAL CARE FOR THE BLIND

"You see, you write from left to right, but we have to write from right to left this way. We have a much harder job learning our alphabet, too. You only have one to learn, we have two really."

A group of children were gathered round the visitor eagerly explaining how they must adapt themselves gradually to our ways. It was a most casual acceptance of fact—"you can do it this way, we have to do it that way."

Were they foreigners,—Japanese or Chinese children? you ask. No. But theirs was also a strange and different land—the Land of Darkness. They were blind children in a New York public school class.

They showed how they work arithmetic on a special hollow metal slate. They make the digits by placing in different positions in specially cut holes in the slate little lead slugs like those of a printer, one with a raised ledge, the other with two points on top. William volunteered to do some problems in subtraction and long division, working them out with little rows of slugs on his slate.

Carmelo was persuaded to write for the visitor. With braille writing, by means of dots punched with a stylus from right to left so that the raised dots on the other side can be read from left to right, almost everyone is somewhat familiar. Jeanette, the oldest girl, had to reprove Carmelo a little for his spelling, but then Carmelo is only in the 4B and he was writing revised braille abbreviated!

About the two alphabets, Jeanette explained that there is an American braille which public school children in New York used to learn. Recently, because of the multiplication of systems used by different educational institutions and publishing companies, a representative committee decided upon a revised braille for all schools and institutions. Late comers in classes for the blind theoretically need to learn only revised braille, but so many books have been published in American braille that it is practically necessary to know both systems.

The frank and practical acceptance of the fact that in many ways they are like foreigners among us, reading and writing a different language, clears the way for the rapid progress of these children. Marvelously they do the regular work of the school, going to every class, taking down dictation and writing notes in braille, studying from their own texts and working arithmetic in their own way. They spend only their study periods—and periods in drawing and physical education in which they cannot take part—in the class for the blind, where a special teacher helps them with any difficulties. She teaches them typewriting, both on a regular and on a braille typewriter. She interlines their examination papers, translating their braille into script so that the history or geography teacher can correct them. She reads to them, gets volunteer readers from among the upper grade children for them, orders books, explains things that need explaining, talks with their regular teachers and looks after them generally.

Classes for the blind were first opened in New York public schools in 1909, but now such classes are scattered through the elementary and junior high schools wherever they are needed. Transportation or guides are provided free of charge.

At present there is only one class for the blind in a high school, in Wadleigh High School for girls. There again the work of the class teacher is to supplement the regular class work, and also to plan programs and advise as to courses. She must be capable of giving help in anywhere from fifty to seventy high school courses, for her pupils may come from any course and any grade in high school. In addition, she helps the girls plan for the future; she advises for or against college, according to the girl's chances for success; she arranges bazaars to furnish money for dictaphones that she may open up a new field of usefulness for the blind; she continually works on the problem of finding jobs for her graduates because there is no one else to do this necessary placement work.

Sight Conservation Classes

Besides these classes for the blind or children so nearly blind they must learn to read and write braille, there are sight conservation classes in the elementary and junior high schools. Special teachers for classes of twenty or under supervise the study work of children whose vision is very poor or failing, providing notebooks and the few text books available in large print, seeing that the children go to oculists or the clinics when necessary, instructing them in the care of their dim vision, and giving them special handwork that may serve as a background of training for a job.

Sight conservation classes are a recent development. Formerly the schools were content to let the child with poor vision struggle along as best he could, straining his eyes and accomplishing little. Now the schools assign a special teacher in a special class to help him keep up with normal children. These teachers take the utmost pains to conserve his failing vision and if medical attention can better it, then to obtain that medical attention for him. They try to insure his independence when he leaves school by offering him through industrial handwork the rudiments, at least, of a trade training.

A pupil in a sight conservation class must spend even more time than a blind child in the special class, for, having some vision, he will be tempted to use his poor eyes too much in other classrooms which are not specially lighted or equipped. Reading and all written work of any length he must do in his special room. Physical training, arithmetic, spelling and much of history, geography and nature work he can take with the other children in the regular classes.

The staff in charge of blind and sight conservation classes needs many things—more textbooks, better equipment. The staff itself is not sufficient for the requirements of a growing department. A special music supervisor, with a knowledge of braille notation, is one of the things which those in charge think vital to the work with children whose other senses must make up for the lack of one. Class registers from fifteen to twenty grow too large for allowing enough attention to individual children.

The equipment and lighting of some of the rooms that sight conservation classes have had to use still leave much to be desired in the older schools, but these are being gradually remedied. As yet there are not enough texts in large print to supply the sight conservation classes and the teacher must spend a great deal of time in tedious copying into notebooks that serve as substitutes for books.

Provision for sight conservation classes in high school, so that no handicapped child be forced to end his school work without high school is especially needed. For it is a great work that the schools do in giving these children of a near-foreign land a chance to be normal, successful, happy, useful children, growing up with a hopeful outlook for the future.

II. THE UNGRADED CLASS DEPARTMENT

DIFFICULT as are the problems presented by children with physical handicaps, their solution is perhaps easier for the schools than the problems of hundreds of other children whose handicaps may not be so obvious but are none the less severe. In this latter group are children born without the mental ability required for regular school work. In this group, too, are children suffering from mental and nervous disorders about which science knows little and which teachers and principals too often mistake for intentioned misconduct and insubordination. There are also children whom neglect and abuse and bad influence at home have totally unfitted for participation in orderly and happy school life.

The Magnitude of the Problem

These are some of the "problem children" of whom so much is heard lately. How many of them are there? Of those who have been definitely reported, 18,903 were referred to the ungraded class department during the first seven months of the last school year; 695 are in probationary schools, and 287 in the New York Parental School,—a total of nearly 20,000. These figures do not take into account those truants whom the Bureau of Attendance is always trailing, nor children who are referred for special attention and adjustment to visiting teachers in the regular schools. And, doubtless, there are many problem children whom teachers have not reported—problems they themselves are trying to solve or that are not recognized.

Take the first of these groups of handicapped children—those of low mentality. Mental measurements have shown that from two to five percent of the children of school age have not the mental capacity to do the work of the traditional school curriculum. It is estimated that ten percent of the amount spent on education annually in this country is spent in an unproductive effort to re-teach children what they have failed to learn in one school term. New York City would thus apparently contribute to this fruitless effort $11,000,000 annually. Formerly this group of handicapped children was simply carried along in school; they studied in one grade two terms, then were pushed along to another teacher, and so on for long weary years until they were old enough to quit or troublesome enough to be transferred to a probationary or parental school. The schools were giving these children a fifth grade education for which a twelfth grade rate was paid—or the price of the whole elementary and high school education of a normal child.

At the end of 1925 the city school records showed 262,177 children retarded in school, approximately fifty percent of whom were retarded more than one term. Mental measurements again have proved that a large percentage of all children who are overage for their grades are of low mentality—that they have failed because they could not do otherwise working with the traditional curriculum.

The presence in school of even a few problem children makes the task of the teacher infinitely more difficult and operates against the welfare of all the other children in a class. The children themselves, continually scolded, continually discouraged, become morose, destructive, sullen.

They come to hate school and teachers and are ready whenever a chance presents itself to break into mischief which may develop into vice and crime. Realization of these facts led to the establishment in 1906 of the Ungraded Class Department.

The functions of the Department of Ungraded Classes are two-fold: (1) the examination of problem children, and (2) the organization and supervision of instruction in the ungraded classes.

THE PSYCHO-EDUCATIONAL CLINIC

For the first of these functions, the examination of children sent to the department by principals and others throughout the city, a psychological and educational clinic is maintained in which the children are given physical, psychiatric and psychological examinations. These examinations are supplemented by facts about the child's family and his personal history.

The personnel of the clinic staff is made up of trained workers from four different fields,—education, psychology, medicine and social work. The psychologist examines the child to determine learning capacity and notes, as she examines, habits or traits that suggest certain aptitudes or inaptitudes, and certain emotional or unemotional reactions. Children who show signs of extreme mental or nervous disorders or whose cases present particularly difficult problems are turned over to a psychiatrist. A psychiatrist is a scientifically trained physician who deals chiefly with nervous and emotional troubles. The visiting teacher, who has had training and experience both as a teacher and as a social worker, makes contacts with the child's parents or with any of the social or welfare agencies that she knows may help him.

The demand by principals for the services of the clinic are far in excess of its facilities. Of the 18,903 children reported for examination, the clinic has been able to examine only 9,238.

Here is an overgrown boy, overage for his grade, referred by a principal after a wild outbreak in which he tore up his teacher's roll book. This violent act of resentment at a teacher's criticism of his work may mean a mental disorder that makes it unsafe for that particular boy to be in school. That is for the psycho-educational clinic to find out.

Here is a bright boy who wants to quit high school. His father appeals to the department to try to make some school adjustment that will help keep him in school. A change of course of study, an intelligent interest in his career, may do the trick. One of the three visiting teachers assigned to ungraded classes will probably try her hand at the adjustment.

A mother reports a boy in 3B who is always left back; the clinic discovers that the boy has mental powers only for the first grade work—he will doubtless go to an ungraded class where with special help and special work he can be made to feel the thrill of doing some task successfully.

There are cases of sex offenses reported by principals and assistant principals; cases, too often, of incipient insanity which must be taken from the regular schools for the sake of other children as well as of themselves.

Of all problems that are submitted to the clinic for examination only about one-third may be cared for in the ungraded classes which are the other concern of the department. The troubles of two-thirds are due to causes other than low intelligence. Re-classification in a higher or a lower grade better suited to their abilities takes care of many; sometimes examination reveals that a sight conservation class or a class for the deaf is the place for a particular boy or girl. Cases of other physical handicaps and malnutrition are recommended for special care. Some children's troubles may be dissolved by providing opportunities for natural social activities.

A definite need has been felt in the high school for psychiatrists and psychologists to make scientific examinations of children who are experiencing unusual difficulties either in their school work or in their social relationships. The staff of the clinic has helped where it could, but of course it is inadequate to meet the need of thirty-eight high schools.

Unfortunately, the schools offer at this time no solution for the problems of some children. Children whose mental age is below that of a five-year-old child and children of thirteen years with I. Q.'s of 50 or under are excluded because the schools as now organized can do nothing for them. The school of the future will doubtless provide sensorimotor training for the group.

There is another sad little group of children to whom the clinic dedicated a half day a week last year—the children from the classes for the physically handicapped, who present special problems of learning or of conduct. Of fifty-two such children forty percent were recommended to ungraded classes; seventeen percent were found to be uneducable.

The Ungraded Classes

In 1926 there were 361 ungraded classes with a register of 7,220 children. What can the schools do for these 7,220 children who cannot do the work of the regular grades because their minds are incapable of grasping all that is required of normal children of their ages?

Much of the work of the school curriculum has to do with the manipulation of symbols, but inability to work with symbols does not necessarily mean inability to work with materials. Therefore the ungraded classes can furnish materials to work with, can develop certain practical skills that may prove useful and that may lead later to an understanding of symbols connected with the practical job. Arithmetic may seem a hopeless jumble of meaningless figures until a boy tries to make a shelf and finds that he has to measure, and that symbols on a ruler will help him in that practical task.

Classrooms for ungraded class pupils are specially equipped with movable furniture so that seats may be often put to one side and study by means of action substituted for the study of symbols. Other equipment deemed necessary includes sewing and embroidery materials for girls, sand trays for small children, looms for weaving, work benches, and horizontal bars for exercising. The cost of equipping an ungraded classroom is about $600,—$216,600 for the 361 classes. Classes accommodate twenty or twenty-five in a room. But remembering the $11,000,000 figure and remembering the fifth grade educations at twelfth grade rates under the old system, that figure seems trifling indeed. For these children, once they have received a fifth grade education, if they are capable of receiving a fifth grade education, will be sent on to the adjustment classes of the junior high schools where many of them will learn the practical foundations of a trade.

With a small group of children an ungraded class teacher has time to search out the individual difficulties of her

UNGRADED DEPARTMENT

pupils. She receives a report from the clinic of each child's showing on the psychological examination so that she may learn what are his greatest difficulties. She has time to experiment with all sorts of devices for spurring interest and awakening the tiniest spark of intelligence. She arranges all the self-expressive activities she knows—dramatizations, songs, painting, drawing, story-telling, rhythms and dances, bench work and handwork of all kinds.

She aims to give her children the essential skills in arithmetic and reading. Reading is the subject with which retarded children have most difficulty. She makes use of every opportunity to have the child associate the symbol with the familiar object and of every situation in the classroom that requires his ability to read. Finally she adapts her reading lessons so that they demand a motor response —run, jump, toss the ball, pick up the book,—so that always symbols shall be impressed on the memory by a practical demonstration of their meaning. Re-examinations of ungraded children show frequent examples of improvement.

The supervisors of the department are consultants with whom the teachers may talk over problems of subject matter, method and analysis of children's difficulties. The teachers are given opportunity to visit, with the supervisors, classes presided over by superior teachers, so that new methods may be discussed and demonstrated.

A type of ungraded class which is unique in school organization is maintained at Bellevue Hospital. These classes are for the psychopathic and psychotic children who come to the attention of the department of ungraded classes. They present a problem to the parents and to school officials which is greater by far than the problem presented by children of low intelligence. Certain children who have suffered from the dread disease encephalitis or "sleeping sickness" are sent to this class. They are known as "post-encephalitic" cases. They present behavior problems which are often mistaken for incorrigibility. They baffle physician and teacher. The work of these classes has already demonstrated that constructive work with these afflicted children is a necessary part of the modern school system.

The clinic comes in again for re-examination of children in the ungraded classes whenever they are recommended either for a transfer back to the regular classes or when they are old enough to leave school and apply for working papers. Some schools issue to ungraded class children leaving school a "certificate of merit."

The Future of the Department

The above heading is used in place of the often re-iterated Plans for Future Development because the department has already worked out very definite figures on the department's needs in order to accomplish even the two functions set for themselves. There are those 10,000 or more children reported to the clinic for special care which the clinic is not equipped to give them. The department estimates that this job could be finished if twenty-three trained people were added to the staff, seven assistant inspectors, ten psychologists, four visiting teachers, and two medical inspectors.

It is estimated that for the proper supervision of the ungraded classes seven additional inspectors are needed. There are now three supervisors of ungraded classes who act as consultants with the teachers in modifying courses of study and methods of procedure in a pioneer endeavor, for as yet there have been no standards established for the work of an ungraded class.

Since 1918 the department has been housed in old buildings with neither adequate space nor suitable equipment to carry on the work of the department. The department dreams of a time when it may have a suitable building—A House of Understanding—to which all problem children who need such attention may be referred for examination, kindly interest and scientific treatment.

III. SPECIAL SCHOOLS FOR BEHAVIOR PROBLEMS

PROBATIONARY SCHOOLS

MANY of the problems handled by the visiting teacher are, of course, problems of behavior, but there are by no means enough visiting teachers to take care of all behavior problems, nor can visiting teachers alone give to certain types of problem children the special kind of education and treatment that is needed throughout the school day to train them in the paths of orderly and useful citizenship. Children who are continually holding up the work of a class because of extreme misconduct and feats of mischief or worse are an ever present problem to teachers and principals. Many educators feel that they should be separated from the regular classes, partly because teachers have no right to take time from a whole group of pupils to discipline one or two unusually troublesome children, and partly because the troublesome children themselves need special help and attention throughout the day which a busy classroom teacher has not time to give.

The principal of P. S. 120 Manhattan, which was the first probationary school in the world, declares that at least fifty percent of the boys who are transferred to probationary schools are as abnormal as are neurotics, cripples, mental defectives and all the other special class children. Not abnormal physically or mentally, perhaps, but temperamentally abnormal. She feels that they are as much in need of special instruction and expert care throughout their school days as are those other children with more obvious defects—the blind and the deaf and the crippled.

P. S. 120 was established twenty years ago to give this special care in a regular day school to boys of neighboring East Side schools who were "in trouble" of one kind or another. It's aim was not to punish past wickedness but to prevent future delinquencies. There are now two probationary schools in the city—P. S. 120 with an annex at P. S. 37, Manhattan, and P. S. 61, Brooklyn.

The aim of these schools is to prevent future delinquencies by substituting good habits of industry, courtesy and decency for bad habits the boy has begun to form. He is to have an entirely new chance. They examine him carefully to see where he belongs in school and to find out, if possible, what special interests or aptitudes he may have. He is given intelligence tests and achievement tests and placed in the proper school grade according to the findings. He is given a physical examination and all effort is made to have any defects that may be working against his best interests corrected.

He is expected to measure up to the standards of the regular schools in the essential academic subjects, but the course of study is carefully modified so that academic work may always be approached from a practical point of view. Many of these boys have an aversion to book work but a liking for practical jobs. They like to hammer and saw, to paint and build. And they can overcome their aversion to book learning when they find out that it may be quite necessary to carrying out a practical project. Even fractions are interesting when a fellow has to use them to get his measurements right for a checker board that has been ordered by the Soldiers' Hospital. A little figuring is not so bad when you are making a cupboard to fit above your mother's sink. Reading, geography, history,—all these make more sense when they are tied up to things a boy already knows.

So it is that the probationary schools devote practically a half day to manual training, drawing, shops and physical training which exercise hands and bodies more than heads; and the other half day to academic studies closely connected with the work of the first half day. Moreover, the work done in the shops—printing, woodwork, etc.—is made obviously practical. The boys do printing for the school and for the Board of Education. They fill actual orders from the Red Cross, the Soldiers' Hospital, and from their parents and friends. They sell these things for actual money which is promptly re-invested in materials and equipment for the school. There is usually a Christmas sale of sewing baskets, waste baskets, vases, and the like made in the manual training rooms. One year P. S. 120 sold more than $1000 worth of articles the boys had made.

P. S. 61, Brooklyn, has a canteen in charge of the boys run on a slight profit basis. The boys in charge do all the actual work, the buying, planning, figuring and management under the supervision of a teacher, and the other boys patronize. The school bank is also made into a practical business run in connection with a course in business methods. Both schools maintain school magazines written and published by the boys.

Principals and teachers in these schools make use of every known device for fostering a school spirit of enterprise, pride in accomplishment, loyalty, and fair play. In P. S. 61, for example, the boys are organized in companies with captain and lieutenants and there is keen competition over company records. Any boy who breaks a school rule spoils his company record and so is made responsible not nearly so much to his teachers as to the rest of the boys.

Do the probationary schools get results? Five years ago, an after-career study of the alumni of P. S. 120 showed that eighty-three percent of them had definitely made good and the remaining seventeen percent included all those boys of whom no record could be found. Only a few of the 9,000 boys who have been in the school have been known to have a criminal record later.

There used to be an idea current that boys could be more or less miraculously "reformed"—that one could take an erring boy, punish him, train him for a few months in the way he should go and he would be a good boy ever after. Then he was returned to the same conditions which had contributed to his former delinquency—poor home conditions unremedied, perhaps—to old associates, to schools where mass teaching is the only teaching possible, and in most instances backsliding into the old ways was inevitable. The task of a probationary school, on the other hand, is not to punish nor to reform by miracles but to prevent by sustained constructive effort—to prevent the formation of unbreakable bad habits, and to implant in their stead abiding good habits. To do this it is not sufficient that a boy stay in a special school for a few months but he must stay until his teachers are satisfied that his good habits will keep him straight even in the old environment.

Adjustment Schools

The probationary schools are for boys. Girls, of course, often present behavior problems, too, but the regular schools struggle along with them as well as they can, sometimes transferring them to special classes where trade work is taught, sometimes to certain schools which offer special opportunities and which are better equipped for handling "problems" than others.

Many principals feel that children who present behavior problems should never be segregated from the influence of normal children in any case and especially that they should not be allowed to feel the stigma of public disgrace. In response to this feeling several so-called adjustment schools have grown up which take the most troublesome behavior problems, girls and boys, from neighboring schools and try to fit them into a regular school.

They give the child work with children of his own age in physical culture, shopwork, etc. They work up lagging academic studies by special tutoring and give to each child's failings individual attention. Homes are visited, but usually without the aid of trained workers, in an effort to help out there if conditions are against the child.

Only teachers imbued with a true missionary spirit can do all these things, for they must do harder and more particular work and carry more responsibilities, with no more financial compensation than the ordinary teacher. They are conscious of the risk of giving a preponderance of attention to the problem child at the expense of the "law-abiding" child, and try to offset that risk by extra effort and longer working hours. To avoid classification as probationary schools, the adjustment schools forego many probationary school advantages, such as the higher salary schedule, limited classes, and special shop equipment.

Detention Schools

Two annexes of P. S. 120, Manhattan, one in the main building of the Society for the Prevention of Cruelty to Children on East 105th Street and one in the Bronx building of the Society, take care of still another group of children with special problems. These are children held in detention homes—some of them delinquents, others merely the victims of parental delinquency and neglect.

Six teachers in the 105th Street building preside over rapidly changing groups of pupils who belong anywhere from the first grade to the fourth year high school and who may stay in the detention home only a few days or possibly six months or more. Every room has a widely assorted group of pupils, ten to thirty of them at a time. Classification of pupils in this strange school is made according to the conditions of their stay there. If a child is a delinquent he is put in an A, B or C division according to the gravity of the offense for which he is being held; if not, then into a division with the more tractable children.

Necessarily the tasks of a teacher in a school of this kind are never two days alike. The school authorities have not thought it right to allow these children to spend several weeks or months without the benefits of school; yet they cannot allow them in the regular schools until the courts have decided what is to be done with them. The teachers assigned to detention schools must do what they can for each individual, keeping him up to the academic work of the grade in which he belongs as well as possible and giving him whatever other work he may like or which may prove useful to him.

Much handwork—drawing, weaving, cutting—sewing and millinery for girls and woodwork for boys is offered.

Some of the children have never been to school; many come with no school records to help the teacher place them. Texts in French, German, Italian or other languages are sometimes needed, for these children may be eighteen years old and unable to speak or read our language.

Discipline must be carefully maintained and the teachers are never free to leave their classes unattended. Yet, throughout the school the aim of the teachers is to interest these children, to help them, to make them forget any disgrace and misery that may have gone before, and to give them standards of courtesy and decency and social intercourse. Many come from homes sadly lacking in any standards whatever, and the cheerful school rooms of the detention home with their movable furniture and their plants and gay paintings, drawings and stenciled curtains, may be the only pleasant rooms the children have ever known.

Up in the Bronx one teacher suffices. She teaches the boys of the home in the morning, the girls in the afternoon. Her children are there an average of one week only, although occasionally a child stays much longer pending the settlement of his case in court.

The building is old—it has no outdoor playground, it is crowded, the schoolroom at night becoming the boys' dormitory. But against all these odds teacher and matron strive—and in some measure succeed—in giving these children at least a memory of better things than they have known before and an inspiration to try to live up to some of the things they have learned there. Sometimes letters come back telling of this boy or that girl who is deeply grateful for his or her memories and inspiration and who is started on the right path again.

THE PARENTAL SCHOOL

The children in the detention homes and many of those in the Parental School are children whose problems have been put in the hands of the courts and who are in a measure out of the hands of the school. Some boys are sent to the Parental School directly by the Director of the Bureau of Attendance with the consent of their parents, but if the parents object and the Director feels that the Parental School offers the only solution of the problem, then he will ask that the boy be committed by the courts.

The aim of the Parental School, which consists of a number of cottages and a large administration building on a beautiful hilltop site of 107 acres in Flushing, is to give boys who have become habitual truants and who have been unable to get along in the regular or other special schools education and maintenance in an atmosphere that will make for the formation of good habits of industry and orderliness. To do this the boys are assigned in groups according to their ages to one of the fifteen cottages, each of which is in charge of a man and his wife. When new cottages now under construction are completed the school will accommodate 490 boys in classes of not more than twenty.

The work is of two kinds—three hours a day of school work and three hours of manual work in one of the many shops offered by the school. School work includes the regular academic subjects, manual training such as is offered in the regular schools, and art work. Chief emphasis in the shops is on practical accomplishment. The boys do Board of Education printing in the printing shop; other shops teach tailoring and repairing of school uniforms, plumbing, shoe repairing, auto repairing, carpentering, baking, housework, laundering, farming—all getting the manual work of the school done, and at least teaching useful tasks. School and shop teachers are assigned by the Board of Education.

Boys who have the farm as their shop attend pigs and chickens, and raise fruits and vegetables for the school. Big boys do the heavy work, and the little fellows weed on Saturdays. The school plant is practically self-supporting. A central heating and power plant supplies all the cottages. Food is prepared in a central kitchen and rolled on small trucks through underground passages to the various cottages. The kitchen is one of the shops; boys in each cottage assigned to housework set the tables, scrub the floors, and make the beds under the direction of the cottage matron.

An effort is made to surround the boys with certain niceties of living with which they perhaps never have been familiar before—spick-and-span rooms, white coverlets on the beds, tablecloths, napkins, and growing plants in the dining room windows. But their life is run on military lines; plain severe order rules everywhere. The boys have only two periods a day when they are at all free, an hour before dinner at night and an hour after. And even that hour after dinner seems to be mostly devoted to preparation of school lessons for the next day.

The day goes like this: up at six, a detail job—of cleaning usually—breakfast, another job, school or shop three hours, lunch, school or shop again, supervised athletics one hour, a free hour, dinner, another free hour, and bed. The boys are, of course, under eternal supervision and of necessity at night under lock and key. Religious instruction is offered on Sunday for the various denominations. An assembly is held once a week, when the boys sing and those of special merit receive faculty commendation.

BEHAVIOR PROBLEMS

When a boy has been in Parental School six months he is automatically brought up for parole, if he has been committed by the courts. Many of these boys, like the children in the detention homes, are in trouble as a result of home conditions. Occasionally when these home conditions are too bad a boy is kept at the school a second six months. Many of the boys are repeaters, sent to the school a second term either by the Bureau of Attendance or the courts. Most of them are retarded in school—many of low intelligence. The brightest boys are put into the printing shop and from there the teachers are sometimes able to get them jobs. No provision is now made for following up the boys when they leave the school. The principal asked in the 1927 Budget that a visiting teacher be allowed for follow-up and placement work, but the item was not provided. Those in charge of the school feel that a psychiatrist to examine the children and a visiting teacher to do the follow-up work are absolutely necessary to the proper functioning of a school which is to "reform" boys and give them a chance to start anew on a right path.

It is a debatable question whether or not six months in a school such as the Parental School or in any school is sufficient time to change a boy's habits; certainly a parental school can do little to change the home conditions that are so often responsible. These reflections bring one inevitably to a fresh respect and support of the regular school's preventive work with children who show symptoms of developing behavior problems—through adjustments within the school itself, through the work of visiting teachers in the home and in the school, and through the work of school and vocational advisers who take an interest in individual children.

The Board of Education maintains school classes in a number of other institutions to which the courts have committed wayward boys and girls, such as the Jewish Boys' Protectory and the Cedar Knolls Schools at Hawthorne and the Episcopal House of Mercy for Girls at Valhalla. The aim of the school work in these institutions is to provide the children with a trade by which they may be able to earn a living and lead an independent self-respecting life later if they choose.

IV. EXTENDED PATHS AND BY PATHS

I. VACATION SCHOOLS

THE work of Summer vacation schools, giving pupils opportunities to make up work in which they have failed or which they may have missed, or to secure rapid advancement, is being extended rapidly. Opportunity classes in summer elementary schools have been organized for twenty years but summer junior high school and high school opportunity courses are quite recent. In 1925 an experiment with summer junior high schools established their worth and in 1926 three summer junior high schools gave children an opportunity to make up work in which they had failed. The first summer high school was organized in 1920 and in 1926 the standards established in the six summer high schools were accepted by the Board of Regents as equal to the regular high school standards.

For Elementary School Children

The elementary vacation schools take care of four types of children in the order named:

1. Non-promoted—or hold-overs—or repeaters.
2. Children who need to complete an attendance of 130 days for employment certificates.
3. Overage, bright pupils specifically recommended in writing by their principals.
4. Foreign pupils from all grades who need help in English.

Vacation schools serve a number of excellent purposes and practice a number of excellent economies. First, they cut down the dreadful cost of educating "repeaters." It is estimated that seven times the cost of vacation schools is saved each year by restoring thousands of children to normal progress. Second, they cut down the equally dreadful overcrowding of the regular sessions by speeding up progress of hundreds of pupils. Third, they make good use of an expensive school plant that might otherwise stand idle. Incidentally the encouragement given to many a "leftback" by this chance to make up, and to many an ambitious child by this chance to go ahead, has its ingratiating effect on the pupil's work when he returns to the regular session.

Vacation schools give a six weeks' course five days a week. In 1926 the elementary classes in fifty-three vacation schools enrolled more than 20,000—11,131 hold-overs, 9,320 overage and bright children and 343 foreign children. These classes covered the work in the fundamental subjects of the curriculum from the 4B to the 8B grades and in addition there were twenty-six classes in manual training and thirty in domestic art.

For High School and Junior High School Pupils

The three junior high schools last summer accepted only repeaters. Summer high schools are organized for two types of children—repeaters and those who wish to take advanced work in one or more of the major subjects. Pupils are required to attend at least eighty-five percent of the session in order to qualify for promotion, and at the end of the first two weeks an elimination test excludes all those who have not been consistent in work or record and who have not demonstrated their ability to obtain the coveted promotion.

The curriculum includes the basic subjects of a general or a commercial course. In the subjects in which Regents' examinations are given the requirements of those examinations are made a basis for the courses given. Last summer the work was accepted by the Regents as an equivalent of one term's work in the regular day high school.

For Handicapped Children

The Board of Education does not forget that in vacation time many of the handicapped children—crippled, blind, deaf and tubercular children, and children confined in institutions—will not be free as other children are for play and recreation unless special provision can be made for them. Therefore, under the vacation school department their special training is continued in summer classes. Thirty-six classes were conducted last summer, many in hospitals and institutions, under the direction of specially licensed teachers. The regular school handwork, basketry, story telling, games, and music were continued and there were, in addition, special vacation features such as bus rides, ferry rides, and trips on a sight-seeing yacht generously donated for the purpose. Gardens and nature study had special attention in districts where gardens were possible.

The demand for places in the vacation schools last summer was much greater than the schools could meet. In view of the savings that vacation classes are able to effect their extension would seem to be highly desirable.

II. CONTINUATION SCHOOLS

IT is the recognition that education has to do with all phases of child development and not solely with a narrow scholastic mental development that has caused the period of required schooling to be continually lengthened and the school program to be enriched. Only the bright in books used to be continued in school past a few years of grammar school when the three R's held sway. Then began the movement to keep children in school up to a certain age or through a certain grade by compulsory education laws and to give practical work that would appeal to those not so fortunate as to be able to continue a scholastic career or not fitted by taste or aptitude to the old type of "higher education."

Why Continuation Schools Were Established

In 1910 a law was passed in New York State compelling attendance at evening schools by boys who had not finished grammar school and who were not attending a regular day school. That law, however, was a sad failure and was never fully enforced; its injustice was too flagrant. Boys who worked all day came home at night too weary for more work,—and for many of the boys affected, school was hard work. Parents objected and employers refused to assume any responsibility for the boys' attendance at night school. The New York Academy of Medicine definitely stated that compulsory evening school attendance was bad for the health of the boys. The law never included girls in its provisions. Of 22,000 boys affected only a few more than 7,000 even registered for the night classes and only nine percent attended in 1913.

The City Board of Education, realizing that these young workers who had left school without anything like an adequate education should have another chance, in 1913 organized day continuation classes in a number of coöperating department stores and factories, and in 1917 began the use of school buildings for workers' classes. Attendance on these classes was dependent of course on the employer's permission, but employers too had begun to see the advantages of more and specialized education for their youthful employees.

Finally, in 1919, to replace the unsuccessful and unjust compulsory evening school law, the continuation school law now in force was enacted. This law provides that all children between the ages of fourteen and seventeen—and up to eighteen after September, 1928—unless they have completed a four-year high school course, not regularly attending a day school, shall go to continuation school at least four hours a week; and that unemployed minors between these ages must attend every school day up to twenty hours a week. The law permits the Board of Education to increase the required time for employed children to eight hours a week.

In the meantime, the new schools were to deal with children, many of whom did not want to go to school, and with employers, many of whom did not want them to go. The schools were to have these children only four hours a week, and in four hours to give them something so obviously worthwhile that children and employers should finally accept the new law as a blessing, not a bane.

What the Continuation Schools Aim To Do

Now what can a school which sees a child only four hours a week do? In general, the continuation school aims to give this adolescent child, whose educational advantages have been less than those of many of his contemporaries, guidance based on expert knowledge and careful attention to his individual needs. Such guidance will affect not only his first or his second job but his whole life work. Vocational guidance, educational guidance, health guidance, recreational and moral guidance—all these the continuation school plans to give.

Specifically, the work of the continuation school falls into three parts; vocational guidance—help in finding the right jobs; offering educational opportunities allied to the child's chosen vocation that will lead to his advancement in it; and, finally, oversight of children in industry, to determine and regulate the effect of the job on a child's health, character and outlook on life, and to make sure that sufficient opportunities for wholesome recreation and social intercourse are open to him.

To carry out these aims two types of continuation schools have grown up: one, the neighborhood or general school which all the continuation school children of the neighborhood enter; and, two, the central trade schools to which children who have chosen a certain trade are transferred, once their fitness for that work has been demonstrated in the general school.

Vocational Guidance Work

A child's first job is usually chosen at random. He has had little opportunity to know what the various types of available jobs offer and he usually thinks most about the money he will get and little about the chances for advancement the job offers. He does not know the qualifications necessary for different vocations, nor has he had a chance to discover his own aptitudes. Consequently, he is forced into a juvenile job. His education fits him for nothing else and certain legal restrictions upon hours and conditions of labor still further narrow his choice. Many of these juvenile jobs are "dead end" or "blind alley" jobs,—that is, they offer no experience or opportunities to learn that will lead to a better or more profitable job; and, what is more, they are purely routine and manual, requiring no use even of the very elementary education the child has already had. After a few years in such a job the child, now nearly grown, will suddenly realize that he continues to work for juvenile wages; that there are no opportunities ahead for him in that particular work; and that his experience will help him not at all in getting another type of job at adult wages.

How can the continuation schools help out? They can give him in his four hours a week a chance to try out other jobs in the school itself, to take special training for a future job in industry, and to find another and better job that will exercise what knowledge he already possesses and that will offer him a chance for promotion. They can offer him the help of vocational counselors who know about the various occupations; of teachers who have special knowledge of certain industries; and of placement bureaus whose task it is not only to find jobs but to find jobs in which a particular boy or girl will be able to succeed and advance.

Every continuation school makes one of its major tasks that of helping individual children to choose the right job and the right kind of training for that job. First, there is the teacher who receives the boy or girl in his neighborhood continuation school. This counselor looks over his records—school and job—asks him what he wants to be and what he likes to do and why; considers any physical or other limitations his records may show; and suggests occupations which she, in the light of her special knowledge of jobs and of adolescent children, thinks will suit. In the reception or "reservoir" class the boy learns what the school can do for him and what qualifications are necessary for various occupations. Then he is given a chance to try out in a chosen vocation and the counselor consults with him from time to time to see whether or not he is satisfied and is making progress. If not, he is transferred to another department; if so, he may be transferred to a central trade school or he may continue the course he has chosen in his neighborhood school.

Educational Opportunities Offered

He may choose from the following comprehensive list; if his own neighborhood school does not offer all of these he can be transferred to other schools that do:

Woodworking	Elementary School Diploma	Homemaking
Printing	Civil Service Examination	Office Practice
Machine Shop Practice	French Flower Making	Bookkeeping
Auto Mechanics	Arithmetic	Banking
Garment Design	Civics	Personality
Mechanical Drawing	Stenography	Lampshade Making
Plumbing	Trade Drawing	English
Music	General Mechanics	Hygiene
Sewing and Dressmaking	Jewelry Manufacture	History
Novelty Work	Commercial Art	Accounting
Power Machine Operating	Electric Wiring	Sign Painting and
Salesmanship	Radio Construction	Show Cards
Typewriting	Cooking	
Commercial Law	Hygiene and Home Nursing	
High School Academic	Millinery	

Each of the vocational courses is accompanied by related academic work that will be useful to him on his job. Instruction in all continuation school classes is of necessity individual. Its task is to guide individual pupils into paths that will start them right for *life*. Therefore, every pupil must be allowed to go in the way that is best for him. This individualization of school work is provided by the use of job instruction sheets which are put into the hands of a pupil for him to accomplish, first, on his own initiative, and then with the help of the teacher. A class usually presents twelve jobs to be done before the pupil can go on to another class. His job instruction sheet will set forth clearly just what each job is, why it is included, to what it is leading, and how it may best be done. This plan reminds one of the Dalton contract plan although it was developed independently, and it works in the same way by allowing every student to progress at his own rate of speed. The ambitious may plough ahead rapidly; the slow pupil is never left back; and yet competition stimulates action.

Specialized Central Continuation Schools

The neighborhood schools offer try-out courses in which a child may learn about a number of trades, trade preparatory courses which directly train the child for the trade he has chosen but is not old enough to enter, and trade extension courses in which he may get instruction in the trade he is already following. But in the last two or three years the central trade schools have been organized to meet a very logical and definite need. It is essential that the schools have more and better equipment for this trade extension function, especially in the more common and more highly skilled trades. It is essential that there be provided courses of study based directly on the needs of industry, teachers experienced in the trades, and shops that will offer conditions similar to those of the industry itself.

The central schools already organized include:

The Printing Trades School

This school is a splendid example of employer, trade union and school coöperating for the good of young employees. The employing printers of the city and two of the printers' unions have equipped one floor of the building at 240 West 40th Street with $165,000 worth of printing equipment, and, in addition, they pay the difference between the salary offered to trade teachers by the Board of Education and the union scale, thereby allowing the school to get expert teachers directly from the trade.

The school authorities working with a Joint Apprentice Committee from the trade have made a course of study, including (1) work in English, mathematics and industrial hygiene for practical application to the printing trades, and (2) actual practice at various types of work connected with printing—type setting, composition, proof reading, operation of presses, etc.

The Commercial School

The Central Commercial School on one floor of a loft building, 725 Broadway, looks like the offices of a thriving business. This school is offering, with special equipment—much of it donated by manufacturing companies—and with special teachers, courses in office practice, calculating machines, salesmanship, commercial art, bookkeeping, stenography, typing, and related subjects.

The Building Trades School

A new school is just being equipped with the necessities of the building trades.

The Needle Trades School

An advisory committee of people prominent in the needle trades is helping with the course of study and equipment of this new school.

PLACEMENT AND FOLLOW-UP OF THE PUPIL ON HIS JOB

Each school has its placement bureau in coöperation with the State Labor Department or the Vocational Service for Juniors. These bureaus are able to find suitable places for practically all who apply. Twenty-four thousand placements were made by them in 1925–26. Unemployment among minors of continuation school age has steadily decreased since the establishment of the placement bureaus. In 1922, ten or twelve percent of minors of continuation school age were unemployed; in 1925 the percentage of unemployment was less than five percent; in the first half of 1926 only two percent—a much smaller percentage than for the whole group of unemployed of all ages. And this in spite of the fact that the Board of Education has not provided teachers enough to make it possible to enforce that provision of the continuation school law requiring that those who are out of employment attend school twenty hours a week instead of four. The State Department of Education recommends that the Boards of Education make special effort to enforce this provision because of its conclusion that unemployment will be still further reduced thereby.

Wages paid to continuation school pupils range from four dollars a week—in a trade where it is still customary that apprentices pay for their training—to sixty dollars a week. The median wage is fourteen dollars. Every job is, of course, investigated before a child is put into it, and in many cases illegal employment of minors has been discovered and stopped. Whenever it seems advisable the placement bureau will try to find a better job for a boy or girl already employed—one that will offer him more chance for advancement or that will utilize the work he has done in continuation school.

In order to know exactly how its pupils are faring in the business world, and in order to secure the invaluable help and coöperation of parents, employers and business leaders, a system of follow-up of pupils' careers by the teachers of the continuation schools has been established. Each teacher is required to devote an hour a day—much too short a time—to the task of coördinating school work with the job and with the home. The teacher usually spends this daily period visiting pupils' homes or employers—homes where it is thought that parents can help, employers when a teacher wants to find out how a child is progressing on a job, what that job offers, and how the employer feels about continuation schools. Sometimes the purpose of the teacher is to convince the employer that the continuation schools are really giving his employee valuable training and to enlist his support and help. Moreover, by means of information the teachers glean from these visits to offices and shops, the courses of study can be checked and kept up to date to meet changing conditions in the trades.

All the continuation schools carry on correspondence with employers about the children's work—correspondence designed to let the employer know what the schools are doing and at the same time to find out how well a certain boy or girl is doing a job. Employers are invited to visit the schools and make criticisms and suggestions. From employers the response has been prompt and gratifying. Many employers have sent representatives to visit the schools; many do offer advice as to work that would be valuable for their young employees; a great many report on the progress of continuation school pupils in their offices or shops and express appreciation for the help that continuation schools are giving those pupils.

Social and Welfare Work

One of the tasks with which the continuation schools have so far been able to do little because of lack of facilities is that very important one of offering young workers some constructive help and suggestions for the advantageous use of their leisure time. Children of continuation school age are impressionable, easily influenced by the "gang"; easily led, too, in the paths of idealism. The continuation schools encourage the formation of dramatic clubs, glee clubs, school orchestras, and hiking clubs, and the publication of school magazines. They encourage their students to form good reading habits. Nearly every class in the East Side Continuation School, for example, is taken to the New York Public Library where a skilled librarian explains the use of the library.

One outstanding feature is the health program recently inaugurated in the West Side Continuation School under which every pupil is to receive a systematic examination by competent physicians. Four physicians from the Board of Health, together with dental and other special service obtained through the Public Education Association and the Public Health Committee of the New York Academy of Medicine are making a careful study of the aims, methods and standards of model health service for continuation schools. A visiting teacher has also been provided to work with children who present unusual problems of personality or behavior.

Plans for Future Development

In view of the fact that continuation schools have been in existence only since 1919, and that they are a wholly new type of school, taking upon themselves an entirely new job for which no courses of study have been laid down, the program outlined above suggests many lines of future development. But all plans for the future are subject to provision of increased facilities for continuation schools.

The continuation schools were all started in old school buildings or in parts of loft buildings or private establishments. These buildings naturally lack proper facilities. Only one school has a gymnasium available. Not one has a proper lunchroom; rest rooms are rarely adequate. Some schools can never have an assembly because they have no auditorium. The shops are often too small and insufficiently equipped. And yet since the continuation schools are vocational in character their success depends greatly on variety of well equipped shops. New trades should be offered; old ones kept up to date—and that takes money for new equipment.

More important by far than equipment, even in a vocational school, is the teaching corps. The continuation schools experience great difficulty in getting enough trained teachers to do their work, and are forced to use a disproportionate number—nearly twenty-five percent—of substitute teachers. No special license for continuation school teachers has been required by the Board; principals have had to select their teachers from existing lists and then persuade experienced ones to transfer from the regular day schools to a new type of school where they would get no more money but many more new problems. To lure teachers from among the most capable and intelligent workers in the trades themselves, persuade them to take the necessary pedagogical courses, and to work for a salary lower than the union wage scale is almost impossible.

In order that the continuation school teachers have some special training for their jobs, it has been necessary to require them to take outside courses in the special technique suitable to continuation school work and in the organization of occupational subject matter into practical job instruction sheets. And, in addition, many of these teachers, spurred on by enormous enthusiasm for the new job, have elected to take numerous unrequired courses.

The Director of Continuation Schools and his staff feel that, in addition to the teaching staff, there should be specially licensed persons for the tasks of vocational guidance, placement and follow-up work; that for work that has been so little standardized, there should be specially trained supervisors.

When they have received all these things they have many plans for future development—new courses, new recreational advantages, an extension of the health program, etc., etc. For the continuation school is new and dangles before the eyes of educators, citizens, employing business men and labor leaders enormous possibilities for guiding thousands of young citizens into more useful and better paths than, unguided, they might choose for themselves.

III. EVENING SCHOOLS

THERE is no feature of school life in New York City more gratifying than the hum of industry that may be heard on the first three nights of the week from any one of 110 evening schools from the middle of September when school opens until the end of June when school closes. Nor is there any feature more suggestive of the huge task confronting New York schools which must educate not only the usual school population of boys and girls during the day, but also from 35,000 to 50,000 foreigners who annually attend evening schools to learn this country's language, customs and citizenship requirements; thousands of adolescent children who have been forced by circumstances to leave school before their education could be finished; and still more thousands of grown-ups whose ambition sends them to school at night after a full day's work on the job.

What the Evening Elementary Schools Offer

Seventy elementary schools with an average attendance of 30,000 offer three separate types of schooling:

1. A four year course in English, allowing the foreign born man or woman to learn English, acquire an elementary school education and qualify for admission to evening high school.

2. A short course in naturalization.

3. A course in the regular elementary school common branches for those who want to finish their elementary school education and qualify for admission to evening high school.

Here a young Russian immigrant who has never been to school in his life may come 114 nights a year, learn to talk and to read English and study American history and civics. If he is ambitious some public school will be open to him year after year until he has had a chance to go through either a trade school or a high school, and, if he likes, college. If he wants very much to become an American citizen, he may, as soon as he has learned to read and write, enroll in a naturalization class, learn how to get his first papers and supplement his knowledge of American history and government so as to pass the required tests for citizenship.

WHAT THE EVENING TRADE SCHOOLS OFFER

Here a young German or Polish lad, whose parents were unable to send him to school after he was old enough to work, may continue his education from where he left off in a day school right through high school or trade school,— and on to college if ambition takes him that far, for most of the metropolitan colleges offer hundreds of night courses. Restricted immigration is lightening the task of evening schools to some extent, but there are still 800,000 foreigners under twenty-one years of age in New York City; and many of the foreign born who attend public school classes belong to the non-quota groups—foreigners in America on a six-months' visit planning to await their turns to come in with the quota groups from their countries.

And what will this young German or Russian or Pole or Italian or Hindu find awaiting him after he has earned his elementary school certificate? Suppose he wants to learn a skilled trade; or suppose he wants to learn more about the trade in which he is already engaged. He may go to anyone of twenty or so evening schools where trade courses are given and find almost any course he may have set his mind on,—applied electricity, gas engine mechanics, brick laying, cabinet making, fancy plastering, catering, commercial photography, photo engraving, any phase of the printing trade, manicuring and shampooing, ship building or ship fitting, steam engineering, wireless telegraphy, shop and mill mathematics—to mention only a few selected at random from the list offered in the catalog on evening trade schools. Murray Hill Evening Vocational School offers an excellent course in upholstering, and another in painting and mural decoration.

For the textile industry, for example, he will find training in every branch of the trade—textile chemistry, physics, designs of various kinds, needle trades, pattern drafting, machine operating, dress design, dyeing and loom working. He will be trained not just as an operator, but to be a foreman, a leader of the trade. Proper machinery for conducting these varied technical courses is often furnished by the firms who wish their workers to be trained in the schools.

Average attendance at evening trade schools is around 10,000, register 13,000. Information as to the location of the evening schools, the courses offered, time of registration, and length of term has been concisely set forth in the catalog of the evening schools which may be had at the office of the Director of Evening and Continuation Schools, in the Board of Education building.

Special courses for apprentices in several trades have been arranged with committees representing employers and labor unions in that trade. The employee's advancement on the job and in the union is made dependent on his attendance and his progress in the evening school course. Approximately twenty percent of pupils attending evening trade school are apprentices in the trades they are studying.

There is a waiting list for many of the trades, because evening school accommodations are not adequate to take care of them at the beginning of the term; in the fall of 1926 four hundred were on the waiting lists for plumbing courses. The automobile trade courses also have long waiting lists. However, mortality in evening school is large; twenty-five percent will probably drop out before the end of the semester and men on the waiting lists will be moved up to take their places. Thus, in spite of the falling off in the original register, there are at the end of a semester approximately the same number of classes as at the beginning.

Registrants in the evening trade schools and trade courses in high school are mostly between the ages of sixteen and twenty-one, but some courses attract older men. In the building trades, for example, one finds older workers studying blue prints and estimates.

Probably thirty percent of the evening trade school teachers are employed in the day time in the trade they teach, and most of the rest are day school trade teachers.

What the Evening High Schools Offer

Strange to say, evening high schools in New York preceded day high schools. As far back as sixty-five years ago City College began offering secondary education in an evening high school for men. Then came old Brooklyn evening high school—next to the oldest high school in the country—but not until 1876 was there a regular day high school in the city. The old high schools offered subjects, rather than courses leading to some higher school. Most of the high school students were studying for law examinations in those days. Things have changed, for after 1928 in order to have an opportunity to take the Regents' examinations for college entrance an applicant must have gone either to a registered evening or day high school.

After the establishment of regular day high schools and the standardization of high school work the evening schools became for a time merely part-time high schools where students could make up courses they needed for college entrance or supplement their educations in certain needed subjects. But for the last five years the seventeen evening high schools of the city and their several annexes have functioned as regular high schools offering to 30,000 students four periods a night, five nights a week, of intensive work with a diploma for the successful at the end of four or five years.

These evening high school students range in age from fourteen to seventy-one. Many are preparing for college, many more for business, some have purely cultural aims. Most often evening high schools are badly overcrowded at the beginning of the term; many students, of course, drop out later. Some of them are doubtless discouraged by classes where even standing room space is crowded.

Perhaps ten percent of evening high school students complete the four year course. Considering the fact that their school work is added usually to a full day's work on the job, this proportion does not compare unfavorably with that of the day high schools, thirteen percent of whose entrants complete a full course.

The Evening School's Service to the Community

Attendance at evening schools is in round numbers 75,000 yearly. Since practically 50,000 of the 75,000 are taking English and citizenship courses in evening and adult day classes, it is safe to count that number as representing the attendance of men and women from other countries. Figures are available for the year 1924–25 showing the distribution of nationalities:

7,183 Italians	930 Roumanians	3,717 Austrians
8,798 Germans	1,683 Czecho-Slovaks	870 Greeks
2,151 Scandinavians	765 Spanish	2,170 Hungarians
777 Porto Ricans	598 French	10,233 Russians
7,120 Poles	566 Irish	

Jewish people in large numbers are not listed separately but are included under various nationalities. One thousand six hundred and thirty-five negroes, mostly from southern states, included, however, some from the West Indies and elsewhere. There were eleven Indians—native Americans.

The work of the evening schools is one of the greatest Americanization projects undertaken by the school system. It, together with the community centers and forums, offers to the foreigners in the United States competent and free instruction in the language, customs and ideals of the new country to which they have come. It prepares them in a very careful and reasonable way to become good and useful citizens of our country. It offers to their children almost unlimited opportunities for higher education, of which thousands of ambitious boys and girls are taking advantage.

An increased budget in 1926–27 for the evening high schools in particular indicates a realization on the part of school authorities of the importance of offering to the workers of the city ample opportunities for continuing education in the fields of their choice.

IV. ADULT EDUCATION IN DAY CLASSES

SUPPLEMENTING the work of the evening schools in educating the foreign born of the city in our language, customs and citizenship rights and duties, from 150 to 200 day classes in English and citizenship are conducted in various parts of New York's five boroughs. These classes, presided over by specially licensed teachers, may be found in settlement houses, churches, schools, libraries,—in fact in any sanitary room with sufficient light and heat for a class of twenty or more. Attendance must be kept up to twenty or the class lapses.

Purpose of the Adult Day Classes

Here gather Italian mothers who have never been to school before a day in their lives, Austrian doctors with several degrees from European Universities, Chinese students who are ambitious to take college courses once English is mastered, musicians who earn their living playing in orchestras at night, lawyers, professors, waiters, hotel bus boys, all intent upon one thing—learning about America and American ways and above all learning to "talk American."

Go about four o'clock in the afternoon into the basement of Temple Emmanuel at Fifth Avenue and 43rd Street. You will find a number of classes, made up mostly of men of a dozen nationalities and as many stages of culture, pronouncing in unison "America is a republic. Its President is elected by the people. Its laws are made by representatives in Congress. They also are elected by the people."

Many of these men are employed in the downtown hotels and may take an hour in the afternoon to go to school.

Again, stand in the hall outside the "schoolrooms" in the Young Women's Hebrew Association on 110th Street about three o'clock. You hear a babel as of many people talking in tongues. Go into one of the several "schoolrooms" and you will find as eager a group of students as ever you have seen,—this time mostly women, but with one or two men. The women are mostly housewives— mothers who must learn English because little Antony or Manuel at home is getting so that he talks English all the time and Mother can not understand him. They have a time with that tongue-twister "President of the United States." They listen eagerly to the teacher's talk about our government although "government" is quite impossible to pronounce. Talk in this class may often center about "What do you cook for supper?" or "When do you give the baby his bath?" And you may be sure that problems of children's health and school work and playtime come in for their share of discussion. For these women must learn our ways, must know how important promptness at school and attention to notes from principals and teachers may be to their children, must look forward to the time when they, too, will be citizens voting for a President of the United States.

Suggestive of the importance of day classes for foreign women whose home duties are too heavy to allow them time for evening school are State census figures for 1925. There are in New York City 850,000 or more foreign-born women, less than half of whom are citizens. Probably 100,000 cannot read nor write, probably 500,000 are unable to use the English language.

Opportunities Offered by the Day Classes

Some of the day classes for more advanced students are devoted entirely to preparing for citizenship. English and civics are the chief subjects and the mechanics of getting first and second papers is carefully explained. Those who wish may continue in day classes for adults for four years during which time they should have learned the language and have acquired at least the equivalent of a fifth grade education. Usually there are at least two classes in a building so that one may be for beginners, another for advanced students.

Teaching in these classes is perforce of a very special kind. The teacher must be first of all an actress projecting her ideas through graphic demonstrations and exaggerated gestures. The blackboards come in for much use as first textbooks. A number of textbooks are furnished but are of little use until the rudiments of reading, writing and speaking English have been "put over."

The State Department of Education offers courses to teachers of English to foreigners at a small fee in Hunter College, in Hunter College Extension in Brooklyn, and at Columbia University. Many of the teachers are ex-teachers who have married and are willing to teach an hour or two a day. The Board of Education pays for salaries and equipment, but rent for the classes is usually furnished free by outside agencies. Some of the outside agencies pay organizers to interpret the work of the schools to foreigners and encourage them to join the classes.

School work is not always confined to schoolrooms. Some teachers chaperone their oddly assorted groups regularly on outings to places of interest in the city, such as the

American Museum of Natural History, Roosevelt House, the Aquarium, and Jumel Mansion. These trips are followed by the usual consequences when school classes go on an outing—compositions on what the students have seen and heard. Competitions with prizes for the best compositions stimulate interest and effort.

Day classes for foreigners have been established in the city for eleven years. And perhaps there is no part of school work that offers the same return in eagerness, appreciation and joy on the part of pupils as these classes.

V. EXTENDED USE OF SCHOOL FACILITIES

Bureau of Lectures

THE Bureau of Lectures, under the direction of the Board of Education, came before the development of radio and moving pictures. Yet it has lived through the invasion of the movies into the leisure time of the city's people and has maintained a considerable following against that most competent of modern time-fillers,—the radio.

The aim of the Bureau is to provide during the leisure hours of the adult population of the city a program of lectures dealing with practically every branch of human knowledge. It would have been easy enough for such a Bureau to keep its attendance by furnishing lively entertainment—wholesome enough use of leisure time—but it has tried to keep to its original purpose, to induce people to devote some of their leisure time to cultural improvement.

There were maintained in 1925-1926, fifty-seven lecture centers throughout the city. The lectures cover such fields as classic and modern literature, including the drama, with special emphasis upon an intelligent appraisal of present day offerings as represented in such courses as "The Book of the Hour" and "Plays of the Hour;" history, especially United States history, and again with special emphasis upon history in the making, as presented in the "Trend of the Times" courses; sociology and economics, treated in specific lectures and courses and also forming largely the background of discussion in the "Trend of the Times" courses; in art and architecture; in science, hygiene, geography and travel; and finally in music, not from the standpoint of entertainment only, but with a view of covering as wide a range of genuine musical culture as possible, from chants and classic expositions of the dance and the folk song to symphonic renditions of the highest forms of classical music, embracing also the opera in all its forms and including several continuous courses so arranged that they constitute virtually a complete presentation of the history and literature of music.

The centers are widely scattered so that people will not have to go far from home to avail themselves of the lecture courses. The larger centers devote themselves to the sustained courses, such as the "Trend of the Times" mentioned above. Smaller neighborhood centers take lighter subjects, and devote some time to musical and picture entertainments of a high quality.

The Bureau was established in 1888, thirty-nine years ago and was for twenty-nine years under the direction of its founder, Dr. Henry M. Leipziger, who termed it "The University of the People." After the consolidation of greater New York the total annual attendance on the Bureau's courses reached well above the million mark for several years. Then came the forced economies of the war years, and since that time the Bureau has had to struggle along with a fee allowance for lectures—averaging fifteen dollars per lecture—wholly inadequate to secure the type of lecturers a "University of the People" should have.

That the standards of the Bureau have been kept high is due in part to the fact that many lecturers have served at a fee much lower than they would ever accept elsewhere and that many public spirited men and women have contributed their services. One hundred and sixteen lectures were delivered last year without fees, one lecturer giving a course of seven lectures free. Glee clubs, symphony orchestras and musical organizations of various kinds have offered their services gratis or at merely nominal fees.

A few names selected at random will indicate the type of speakers the Bureau has enlisted in the past: President Coolidge, Charles Dana Gibson, Franklin H. Giddings, Booth Tarkington, Charles E. Hughes, W. G. McAdoo, Bishop Manning, General Pershing, Henry Fairfield Osborne, Irving Cobb, Edward Bok, William Howard Taft, and Elihu Root.

The staff of the Bureau consists of the Director, assistant director and local superintendents. The Department of Visual Instruction is also under the direction of this Bureau. The local superintendent at each center must be present to distribute announcements, introduce speakers, take attendance and report on the character of the lectures. The district superintendents of the regular school organization are charged with the supervision of lecture centers in their districts.

Aggregate attendance at the centers in the season 1925–26 was 314,994.

Through the coöperation of the city Department of Plant and Structures the radio has been impressed into service, and the Bureau of Lectures now broadcasts almost nightly at 10:15 from WNYC, and once a week from WEAF. In 1925–26 three hundred and forty-nine lectures and concerts were broadcast, twenty-six concerts were broadcast over WRNY, in addition to the 1,695 lectures delivered at the regular centers.

Lack of sufficient appropriation to allow a higher fee to lecturers and to allow more publicity to be given the courses are effective limitations upon the work of this department. The extension of the use of the Municipal Radio Station, thereby widening enormously the scope of the Bureau's influence is probably one of the lines along which the future development of the Bureau will come. And use of the radio furnishes a most excellent opportunity for the Bureau of Lectures to extend its usefulness and to maintain its original function of instruction and inspiration.

COMMUNITY AND RECREATION CENTERS

Perhaps most extensive in influence of all extension activities is the community center, which makes possible the use of the school plant and equipment by the people of the neighborhood and serves an invaluable end in the amalgamation of races, the rapid transformation of foreigners to Americans, and the fostering of friendship, loyalty, and good will among citizens of a community.

Community centers were started in New York City in 1901, chiefly as athletic and play centers for the youth of the city. Gradually there developed club work, the game room, and the library, and a participation in the development of the community. With the action of the New York Legislature in throwing school houses open to groups of responsible citizens wishing to use them under rules and regulations established by the Board of Education, the community center passed from a recreational movement into one which added a community interest to the work. Club work increased and broadened in its scope and the participation of the adults of the neighborhood rapidly made the community center a real center of community life.

Community and recreation centers play excellent parts in the work of citizenship building and delinquency prevention by providing wholesome occupations for the leisure time of people attending them. Community drama, dances, orchestras, choruses, neighborhood festivals and entertainments, the forum, club meetings, and social gatherings are forms of self-expression which fill a very definite need. This need is especially urgent among wage workers whose daily job is a monotonous and uninspiring grind. Athletic and game competitions are wholesome and healthful for the younger members of the community.

The far-reaching influence of the centers is in a measure indicated by attendance figures. The aggregate attendance in sixty-three official evening centers last year was 3,298,779, which means an average attendance of 447 at each session; in 277 non-official centers 1,304,759, an average attendance of 117. The aggregate attendance in school buildings opened for occasional use was recorded as 308,333, an average attendance of 428 on each occasion.

Attendance at the centers represents a pretty fair cross section of the community. Most cosmopolitan gatherings they are, for within the radius of a few blocks, this cross section may bring in a dozen different nationalities.

The chief material requisites of a center are a well-equipped gymnasium, a well-equipped quiet game room, and a contact with public libraries. More important than these is a corps of properly trained teachers to care for the various groups using the center. After-school centers for children of school age usually have a two hour session from three-thirty to five-thirty o'clock. Permission is often given to groups of parents or to some well-established organization to form a non-official community center in a

EXTENSION ACTIVITIES

school building. This center is carefully supervised by the supervisors of the Bureau of Extension Activities but it may or may not, as circumstances differ, have a teacher assigned to it. Sometimes the Board of Education furnishes such a center with janitorial service, sometimes not.

MEETINGS AND FORUMS

The State education law provides that the schools may be used for meetings pertaining to public welfare, and New York communities take frequent advantage of this provision. Going down the list for the "Extended Use of Schools" in the season 1925-26, one finds such items as these: Boy Scouts Cooking Class, Citizen's Forum, Girl Scouts, Parents' Association, Tennis Club, U. S. Junior Naval Reserve, People's Chorus, Irish Republic, Polish Educational Committee, Russian School, Home and School League, Catholic Big Brothers, Bronx Centers' Association, League of Women Voters, C. C. N. Y. Alumnæ Association, People's Institute, Greek Committee of St. Constantin, Violin Club, Chase Bank Club, Garrick Players, Flatbush Chamber of Commerce, Order of De Molay, Gym Class Teachers Association, and dozens more.

A forum is one of the types of extension activities enlisting the people of the neighborhood. A forum program usually involves the presentation of a topic of current interest by a competent speaker followed by questions and discussion from the audience. That these discussions are sometimes stormy does not detract from their value in educating citizenry.

Playgrounds, Swimming Pools and Showers

The regular health and recreational work of the day school is carried over into vacation periods by the Bureau of Extension Activities which provides trained supervision for playgrounds, pools and showers during the summer months. Vacation playgrounds for mothers and babies offer in many districts the only clean and open space to which mothers can bring their young children away from the wretched heat of a tenement street.

For children of kindergarten age experienced teachers are there to organize games, to give out toys and handwork, to lead in singing and rhythms and to see that the quiet hour is enforced at nap time. Hammock swings in shady places, safe toys which baby cannot swallow or put in his eye, and stations for dispensing milk make the playgrounds suitable havens for the babies,—havens that play their part in reducing infant mortality. Weighing, measuring and examining the babies is conducted by physicians and nurses of the Children's Year Committee.

For the mothers these small playgrounds are places for rest and social recreation,—places, too, where they may receive instruction in the care of children, in nutrition, hygiene, treatment of minor ailments and in standards of physical development. The playground is a meeting place where mothers may come together and plan great things for the benefit of children. Little Mothers, as the older sisters are called, come often in charge of smaller members of their families. To them, too, the opportunities for rest, recreation and instruction are open.

Larger playgrounds are devoted to the older children who must have more space in which to work off excess energy.

EXTENSION ACTIVITIES

The aggregate attendance of the vacation playgrounds in 1925 was 6,550,860. Two hundred-odd playgrounds are open in the summer from one-fifteen to five-thirty; playgrounds for the all day care of handicapped children from nine to five; evening playgrounds from six to eight-thirty; playground annexes from nine to five mostly; and some from one-fifteen to five-thirty. The total of costs for the summer playgrounds with their staff of 1,081 trained people was $254,413.32.

In addition to the regular summer playgrounds the Extension Division has organized play schools for the all day care of children in eleven centers open from eight-thirty to five-thirty. These centers take care of children suffering from improper and irregular nourishment. The play schools have a regular program of food, rest and recreation for the children and instruction in food values and preparation of standard menus for classes of mothers. Through contact with the Department of Health and many outside agencies, hospital or clinic care is provided for children in need of it.

Another of the health activities of the Extension division is the utilization of swimming pools and shower baths in and after school hours. There are twenty swimming pools in school buildings in which evening as well as day classes are conducted by trained teachers of the department. Classes for men and women are held in some schools on alternate nights. Aquatic sports, swimming meets and Public School Athletic League badge tests are conducted in school natatoriums, but since there are not enough most of such meets and tests have had to be held in the municipal pools.

Swimming teachers in schools which have only shower baths and no pool have taken classes to the municipal pools also to learn to swim. The use of the municipal pools is curtailed by the fact that a ruling of the Commissioner of Health does not allow the exclusive use of a pool to any one school or organization. The swimming teachers are especially licensed and selected from a recreation list.

V. KEEPING TRACK OF A MILLION CHILDREN

SUPERVISING AND INSURING ATTENDANCE AT SCHOOL

THE Bureau of Compulsory Education, School Census and Child Welfare, more commonly known as the Bureau of Attendance, is the agency provided by state law by which the schools of the city may get in touch and keep in touch with all the children of school age within its boundaries.

THE FUNCTION OF THE BUREAU OF ATTENDANCE

The duties of the Bureau are to carry out the provisions of the education law with regard to attendance of minors upon required instruction and to maintain the school census.

To carry out these provisions, the Bureau is provided with a staff consisting of a director, an assistant director, a chief attendance officer, six division supervisors, 272 attendance officers, 29 district supervisors, and 110 clerks. The budget of the Bureau for the calendar year 1926 was $973,506.12. However, even this staff has proved to be inadequate to carry out all the duties prescribed for the Bureau. The school census, for example, which is maintained in order to locate every child of school age and to follow up to see that enrollment in school is not evaded, must be carried on for the most part by a house to house canvass. Moreover, the Bureau has certain other duties, in addition to its attendance work, as, for example, the issuance of employment certificates—a duty delegated to it by the Superintendent of Schools. Duties with respect to child welfare are implied by reason of the long title of the Bureau, although there are no specific statutory requirements governing them.

However, the chief function of the Bureau is to enforce the attendance of minors upon required instruction, which means usually attendance at school.

How the Bureau Controls Absence

Within the schools themselves the first step in the control of absence is an accurate record of attendance, which is specifically required of teachers by the state law. The next is to provide for a regular examination of these records by the principal or supervising head, and the requiring of suitable explanations of absence. Accepted excuses for absence are personal illness, death in family, religious observance and severe storm, and, at times, extreme distance from school. The well-organized school controls the greater part of absence by direct dealings with the parents. The attendance officer deals with the parents who do not respond.

From the monthly reports of principals there is compiled and sent to each principal and district superintendent, and the newspapers, a report showing the actual percentage of attendance of each school and its relative rank. This report has been found to be a most useful aid in securing greater regularity of attendance.

The Board of Education through its by-law requires that: "The principal of every school shall report to the bureau of attendance the name of every child absent for unexplained cause, on the beginning of the third day of absence, and of a child absent because of truancy or suspected truancy as soon as the absence is known." The investigation of the causes of absence of such children, the requiring of an appropriate explanation from the parent, the statement to the parent of his lawful obligations—this follow-up work is the principal duty of the attendance officer.

To handle investigations of absence from school, the city is divided into attendance districts, as follows: Manhattan, seven; Bronx, two; Brooklyn, seven; Queens, two; Richmond, one; total, nineteen. Each attendance district is under the supervision of a district supervisor, to whom are assigned a clerk and attendance officers.

Causes of Irregular Attendance

Regular attendance is a product of several factors—the school environment, a child's health and physical condition, his home environment, and in lesser degree the external environment. Where the first three are highly favorable, there is little need for the attendance officer. A child may actively dislike the school, because he is unable to do what is required, or because of dislike of a particular teacher. Parents may be unsympathetic, careless, unintelligent; the child may be handicapped by poor mentality or by a positive physical defect or impairment, and release from school attendance may become the most desirable of things. Forbidden pleasures and undesirable companions may complete the tale. But whatever the cause, absence is the sign. To control absence, first of all, it must be known. Once known, it is obvious attendance officers can deal successfully only with certain causes, and it is their duty to deal with one cause, the parents, the chief factor in the home environment.

How Hearings Are Conducted

After notice to the parent and child and an opportunity for them to be heard, and with the consent of the parent in writing, a child who is an habitual truant may be committed to a truant school for a period not exceeding two years, but in no case beyond the maximum age of required attendance. If the parent refuses such consent, court proceedings may be set in motion against him for failure to cause the child to attend school. If the parent shows, however, that he is unable to control the child, then a petition may be filed against the latter in the Children's Court as a delinquent child.

Hearings are held by the bureau of attendance weekly in the different boroughs for each attendance district and each continuation school district, and parents are prosecuted on a day set aside in certain courts. Six officers of the Bureau are busy all of the time with hearings,—an insufficient number to take care of 23,000 cases yearly.

The following excerpt from "Instructions to Attendance Officers" indicates the spirit in which hearings are conducted. With expert assistance for the making of physical and mental examinations of children summoned to hearings, better use could be made of these opportunities.

"The object of a hearing is not primarily to commit a child to a truant school. Its object is to develop the sense of parental responsibility, to bring about coöperation between the parent and the school, to confront the child with the facts of his irregular habits, and to awaken in him a consciousness of the effects of these habits and consequent desire for improvement.

"A hearing takes primarily the character of an intensive investigation. It is assumed that the motives of the parent are good, and it is *not* to be assumed that the child is bad. Opportunity is taken to find out the nature of the home surroundings, the sense of parental responsibility, and to impress firmly but dispassionately the facts of parental responsibility where it appears to be inadequate. The cause of the failure of the parent to control the child is examined, and better methods proposed, where possible. The relations of the child with his teacher and with other pupils may be gone into, and any specific and motivating sources of irritation uncovered. Inquiry is also made as to his habits, companions, tastes, activities, and places of resort when a truant is absent from school. Principals and teachers should be induced to report fully whatever information they may have concerning the child in these or other particulars, and should be asked not only for the facts shown on the regular reports but for any additional material they may have.

"If for any reason you believe either physical or mental characteristics of the child justify special examination, request that it be made; familiarize yourself with the results of examinations of this character. They are made by the Bureau of Child Hygiene of the Department of Health and the Inspector of Ungraded Classes, Board of Education."

What the Hearings Accomplish

For about one-fifth of the number of hearings held, prosecutions are initiated. The Bureau of Attendance within the school system itself is the final court of appeals in disposing of behavior problems. It is the only school authority which can commit a child to the Parental School, and the

Parental School is at present the last measure of discipline upon which the schools may call.

There are several possible methods the Bureau may take in dealing with these cases:

1. Place the child on probation.
2. Transfer the child to another school.
3. Uphold the principal's suspension from school.
4. Commit the child to the Parental School.
5. Prosecute the parents and later the child.

The great majority of children summoned to hearings are placed on probation under the supervision of attendance officers. While this supervision is largely formal, the result is that most of the children affected are regular in attendance. During the school year 1925–26, 15,043 children were placed on probation. During the same year 744 children under sixteen years of age were committed to a truant school for the first time; 561 were placed on parole, and 202 were returned to the truant school for failing to attend regularly. Forty-six children under seventeen years of age were committed for failure to attend continuation school.

In the hands of the Bureau of Attendance is also the the matter of parole. The Bureau has power to place on parole children committed to the Parental School, although the power is usually exercised only on recommendation from the Parental School parole board. The Bureau of Attendance has no authority over the children it has committed between the time of the hearing and the dismissal or parole.

Maintaining the School Census

Another function of the Bureau is that of maintaining the school census, showing at all times the name, date of

ATTENDANCE BUREAU

birth, names of the parents, and place of residence of every minor under eighteen years of age. Reports from the schools, covering each child admitted, transferred or discharged, supplement the attendance officer's canvassing of his district.

Notice is received from the Commissioner of Immigration of the name, age and prospective residence of each child admitted to the country for residence in New York City, and each case is investigated to make certain the child is registered in school. Certain immigrant children are also admitted by the immigration authorities under bond to attend school, and notice is sent to the Attendance Bureau, which reports monthly to the Immigration Bureau as to the attendance of these children in school.

To insure that every child shall attend school, no child may be discharged from the register of a public school except for duly recognized causes such as transfer to another school or to an institution, expulsion, notice that an employment certificate has been issued, death, marriage, graduation, permanent removal from the city, mental disability, physical disability, quarantine by the Board of Health, etc., etc.

Issuing and Regulating Employment Certificates

The Superintendent of Schools has delegated to the Attendance Bureau the power to issue employment certificates to children old enough to leave school or who have completed certain educational requirements by law. All applicants for employment certificates must pass a physical examination given by doctors furnished by the Bureau of Child Hygiene of the Board of Health. The Attendance Bureau also issues vacation employment certificates to minors between fourteen and fifteen years of age valid for employment when school attendance is not required. Newsboy permit badges are issued to boys between twelve and sixteen years of age, permitting them to engage in the sale or distribution of newspapers, periodicals and magazines after 6 A. M., and before 8 P. M., and outside of school hours.

The Bureau enforces attendance at part-time schools. Employment certificates are issued at continuation schools only, to insure the registration of employed minors at these schools.

The law requires that every minor under seventeen years of age—and after 1928, under eighteen years of age—who is not attending a public, parochial or private school or who is regularly and lawfully employed, and not a graduate of a four-year high school course of study, shall attend a part-time school for not less than four hours a week. It requires also that every minor between fourteen and sixteen years of age, not regularly and lawfully employed, and in proper physical and mental condition, shall attend upon instruction the entire time the public schools are in session, and that every minor between sixteen and twenty-one years of age, unable to speak, read and write English as required for the completion of the fifth year of the elementary school course of study, shall attend a day or evening school for not less than six hours each week.

VI. THE TEACHERS OF A MILLION CHILDREN

I. HOW NEW YORK TRAINS ITS TEACHERS

IN any educational chain there is no link more vitally important to the whole than its teacher training schools. Where does New York get its teachers? From its own training schools mostly, and from surrounding colleges—Hunter College, City College, New York University and Teachers College of Columbia University.

THE TRAINING SCHOOLS FOR TEACHERS

The city training schools for teachers—New York Training School, Maxwell Training School and Jamaica Training School—are controlled directly by the city Board of Education and represent the highest type of education that the Board offers. Training schools are devoted solely to the task of training New York City elementary school teachers. In connection with each there is a model school that serves at once as a demonstration and a practice school. Moreover, all of the schools of the city are utilized as training and practice schools for the three or four thousand young men and women of the city who yearly elect to prepare themselves for the teaching profession.

The oldest of the training schools is Maxwell Training School which began in May, 1885, with forty students and a faculty of four. Training schools for teachers were not then compulsory because high school graduates were eligible to teach without professional training. The course was a one-year course in which the model and practice school played a large part. In 1898 New York Training School came along with a two-year course and finally in 1923 a compulsory three-year course was installed, with plans for a four-year course waiting in the wings only until the three-year course has been well established. The annual register for the training schools is now 5,406, with women much in the majority,—5,147 women and 259 men.

What the Training Schools Give

The three-year course had to be introduced gradually lest there be a sudden shortage of teachers. To anticipate this difficulty certain classes are still being graduated at the end of two and one-half years. The three-year course is based on essential subject matter that is to be taught to the children and on pedagogy. The list of subjects includes, besides the regular arithmetic, English, science, nature study, penmanship, etc., of the elementary school curriculum, such studies as health education, sociology, educational psychology, classroom management, professional ethics, industrial handwork and experimental education. The program is rather rigid with little choice of elective subjects until the last year when students may specialize in a special subject, such as domestic science, or physical education. They may specialize, too, in training for teaching one of three grade groups, the lower, middle or upper grades.

The chief argument for a longer session is that it may allow cultural subjects a larger place in a teacher's training. No foreign language is now taught in the training schools.

To meet the junior high school problem nothing has so far been required of the training schools because junior high school teachers have been selected, except in the case of foreign language teachers, from among experienced upper grade teachers. The problem of training teachers especially for junior high school work has been largely left unsolved. There has been particular difficulty, as has been seen, in attracting teachers of superior training into schools where salaries are less than in high schools.

In the training school program, method and subject matter are taught side by side. Every student spends at least half of her time in practice work and observation of actual classroom work. At least four times during the course of training, students are sent either to the model practice school or into the regular city schools as pupil-teachers to observe and practice teaching. Each model school is a complete elementary school where the city's most competent teachers may give demonstration lessons and where the students are required to teach under the instruction and observation of training school supervisors.

The model schools are not experimental schools. Rather they are regular elementary schools operating under exactly the same conditions as other schools in the city, except that they have picked corps of teachers who also teach student teachers, and that the students are occasionally allowed to conduct classes. At nine o'clock every morning there is a demonstration lesson which student-teachers attend.

When the students are sent into the regular city schools, the principals see that they have a chance to observe the best teaching, particularly of the special subjects and in the grade groups they have chosen, and to teach, either under the supervision of the class teacher or, in case of her absence, in entire charge of a class.

Special demonstration rooms in the training schools themselves give the students an opportunity again for observation and practice. A fine type of demonstration room in the New York Training School has the regular elementary school classroom accommodating thirty or forty pupils on the floor level with seats for the students who are observing at one side on a sloping platform.

In the matter of equipment the New York Training School, in a beautiful new building set high on a bluff overlooking the city at 135th Street and Convent Avenue, is a model. There are specially equipped rooms for every subject,—model flats for domestic science; special cooking, sewing, drawing and nature study rooms; a handsome music room high in the tower; fine gymnasiums with showers and locker rooms, and outdoor basketball courts for the physical training department; an ample auditorium and stage; double unit teaching-demonstration rooms; and, finally, model school rooms where classes from 1A to 6B—and later through junior high school—may be accommodated for model purposes in the building itself. Jamaica Training School is also to have a new building, similarly equipped.

The Standards Maintained

Requirements for eligibility to a training school are: graduation from a recognized high school or equivalent education; completion of certain required subjects such as English, American history, two years of mathematics, two years of science, two years of foreign language, two years of drawing, and two years of music; a satisfactory personality, on the basis of reports from the principal and the teachers of high school; the passing of a satisfactory examination in oral English and a satisfactory physical examination. Through the oral examination the aspirant must convince the examiner that her bearing, her voice, her pronunciation and her personality fit her to become an example to children. The training school course is given full college credit in New York University so that in a few summers a graduate may obtain a college degree.

The pressure upon the training schools to meet the constant demand for trained teachers and at the same time to maintain high standards is one that perhaps allows too little time for new projects, for expansion of curriculum and adjusting of curriculum to meet new demands arising with the development of such new types of schools as the continuation and vocational schools and the junior high schools. The training schools are now crowded to capacity in the effort merely to turn out enough teachers to recruit next year's teaching staff. Whenever this pressure is lessened, the tendency is for the training schools to raise standards and expand courses.

Future Development

The four-year course which has been planned for the future development of the teacher training schools has already been indicated. New York Training School represents the kind of building and material equipment that would seem to be necessary to the proper functioning of the training schools. The need for special training for junior high school teachers is a problem for the training schools to meet as soon as possible.

Still another problem in the minds of the training schools' staff is that of allowing for more experimental work in the training schools themselves and in the model schools run in conjunction with them. The need for experimentation in any school system in order that it be kept up to date, that it be open to new ideas, that its teachers and prospective teachers be allowed to develop initiative and creative ability, is an ever present need. That some of this experimentation be carried on under the expert supervision of the picked and experienced teachers of a training school staff seems a perfectly logical and desirable development—one which will be possible when training schools are not required to give all of their time and resources to furnishing enough competent teachers to fill the gaps in the ranks.

II. EXAMINING AND PROMOTING TEACHERS

ONE of the greatest achievements of the New York City school system is the selection of its teachers by means of competitive examinations. This merit system has been in use for twenty-eight years.

THE EXAMINATION SYSTEM

This system is in the hands of a Board of Examiners, themselves selected by means of a searching competitive examination prepared and conducted under the direction of the Municipal Civil Service Commission by educators in high standing chosen usually from outside the city school system. The Board of Examiners is made up of seven members who have permanent tenure of office.

The Board is empowered to prepare, conduct and grade examinations for all teaching and supervising positions in the city school system except those of high school and training school principals, directors and assistant directors of departments and special branches, district and associate superintendents and the Superintendent of Schools himself.

Examinations may be authorized only by the Superintendent of Schools, upon whom rests the responsibility for seeing that there are enough persons who have passed proper examinations and been placed upon eligible lists to supply the demand for qualified persons to fill vacancies.

When the examinations of the applicants for a certain license have been graded, the names of those who have successfully passed are placed upon eligible lists in the order of the excellence of their passing grades. When appointments are made thereafter for positions requiring that particular license, the choice for any one position must be made from the top three names on the eligible list. The reason for allowing a choice of three names is presumably that there may be certain professional reasons for preferring the second or third on the list to the first. It is customary, for example, to give preference to a person on the eligible list who has been giving satisfactory substitute service in the position under consideration.

Once the examinations for a certain position have been graded and the eligible lists made up in the Examiners' office, the lists are forwarded to the Board of Superintendents to be used in making recommendations for appointments to the Board of Education. Lists are valid for three years only; after three years if those whose names are on the lists have not been appointed they must take another examination in order to be reinstated on the new list.

Types of Examinations

Examinations are conducted from time to time for something like 300 different kinds of teaching and supervisory jobs. To each examiner are assigned certain types of examinations. For example, last year one examiner was assigned to the problem of selecting teachers for vocational schools, evening recreation centers, classes of physically handicapped children and special classes for cooking.

The examination is usually three-fold, consisting of a written paper, an oral examination and either a teaching demonstration, or, in the case of vocational work, a test of practical skill. The examination for which applicants are most numerous is that for License No. 1, to teach any one of the first six school grades. Next in order is the promotion license to qualify for teaching grades seven, eight and nine. The written examination for high school teaching is usually limited to an intensive examination in the particular subject the candidate wishes to teach. There are examinations for principal of elementary school, and for assistants to principals of elementary schools. There are hundreds more for special teachers of all kinds,—kindergartners, teachers of ungraded classes, of classes for the blind, deaf, and crippled, teachers of foreign languages in junior high school, of domestic science, cooking, music, physical education, drawing, and manual training, teachers of trade and vocational classes ranging in variety from bricklaying and plumbing to dressmaking and art jewelry. There are examinations for teachers of probationary and parental schools, for evening school teachers of English to foreigners, for visiting teachers, vocational counselors, playground directors, librarians, and attendance officers.

In the case of License No. 1, the three elements considered in determining an applicant's rating on the eligible list are the written examination, the interview and the applicant's scholastic record. For promotion license the third element is the teaching record. For high school the intensive written examination in the applicant's subject is supplemented by the personal interview and by a teaching demonstration in his subject conducted in a regular high school class by the department head of that school. For vocational and trade teachers a test of practical skill is usually required in addition to the demonstration lesson. A physical examination, it might be added, is given to all candidates to insure their fitness. Wherever available the candidate's record as a teacher is carefully scrutinized and is given much weight in the final determination of his rating on the eligible list.

On the written examinations a system of numbering examination papers conceals the candidate's identity from the examiner marking the papers. In many of the examinations a system is used whereby even the candidate does not know his examination number.

The interview or oral examination is usually brief—not more than a half hour in duration—and is designed to give the examiner a chance to judge of the applicant's personality and ability to use English. Various types of written examinations have been devised, from the old style examination requiring essay-like answers to the more modern short answer tests, where the applicant is asked to mark statements as true or false, complete statements, or to select from a group of several alternative answers the correct one. The new type examinations may be completed and graded more quickly and, moreover, are easily standardized, thereby lessening chance of error in judgment on the part of the examiner marking the paper. Standard answers have been prepared for all examination questions, even those requiring the "essay" answer, to serve as criteria in marking papers.

This problem of devising tests that will be at once fair, comprehensive and brief and that may be carefully graded according to fixed standards is one on which the examiners are working constantly.

Information about examinations is spread to those who may be interested by means of circulars sent to the proper schools in the city or neighboring cities—to teacher training schools and colleges for first license examinations, to the schools themselves for promotion examinations and to outside schools and colleges, if it is felt that qualified persons for certain positions should be attracted to the city. These circulars outline the advantages offered by the positions for which the examinations will be held, including the salary schedule offered, and the qualifications of education and experience prescribed for eligibility to take examinations. In case of trade positions, the examinations are occasionally advertised in the local papers in cities which are the centers of the particular trade for which teachers are needed. Announcements are sometimes broadcast from the city radio station.

It is now the plan of the Board of Examiners, with the consent of the Superintendent, to adopt a fixed schedule of examinations for the next three years so that teachers may know some time in advance when a particular examination is to be held, and that the work of the examiners may be evenly distributed throughout the three years. License No. 1 examinations are now scheduled regularly for June and January of every year. Occasionally, of course, in the case of sudden unexpected vacancies the Superintendent may call for a special examination. Also, the Examiners sometimes give emergency examinations, say, for a substitute to fill a certain position until the regular examination can be held and the position filled from an eligible list.

The seven members of the Board of Examiners find it impossible, of course, to make or to grade examinations for all the types of positions for which they must seek qualified persons; impossible also to do all the work of examination themselves. Therefore, they are empowered to employ to assist them assistant examiners whose names are approved by the Municipal Civil Service Commission, and upon whose services they may call from time to time. These assistant examiners are mostly from the special fields—the trades and such special branches as music, art and commercial subjects—and their aid is enlisted both in formulating tests and in grading them. The Examiners themselves, however, prepare ninety percent of the tests given.

The examiners sometimes allow exemptions from certain parts of an examination. For example, in the case of applicants for reinstatement on an eligible list that has lapsed after three years, they might waive the written examination and use the grading obtained by the applicant on his previous written examination in determining his place on the next eligible list to be prepared. All the other items of the test, of course, would have to be met. Exemptions from some part of the personal or oral examination are sometimes made on college or training school records.

The organization of the Board of Examiners and all details concerning it have been designed to keep that Board an independent body, free from all influence inside or outside of the school system. The aim is to secure an intelligent and absolutely fair selective Board whose duty it is to see that persons properly qualified for certain positions in the school system are given an opportunity to manifest their ability through competitive examinations. For this reason, Examiners are selected by the Board of Education from a list prepared by the Municipal Civil Service Commission; for this reason, too, they are given permanent tenure.

Appeal from the Examiners' Decisions

The decision of the Examiners regarding a candidate is final, subject only to appeal to the State Commissioner of

Education, who has power to reverse or modify their decision. However, the Examiners themselves, realizing that no Board is infallible, have organized appeals committees to which a dissatisfied candidate may present his case.

The appeals committee devised by the Examiners themselves and used last year for the License No. 1 examination is a committee of three members, one of whom is chosen by the Board of Examiners, one by the Superintendent, and the third by the two members thus selected. The Committee is asked to review the candidate's examination and grading and make recommendations concerning it. These recommendations must receive the approval of the Examiners at a regular meeting before they become operative, however. Similar appeals committees have been used in connection with examinations for higher licenses.

III. OPPORTUNITIES FOR TEACHERS IN SERVICE

Opportunities for Continuing Education

OPEN to the teachers in service in New York City are practically innumerable opportunities to continue their education through extension courses. Hunter College, City College, New York University, Columbia University—these are only a few of the educational institutions offering courses especially designed for teachers. Moreover, these institutions are usually willing and anxious to establish courses anywhere in the city if there is a sufficient demand for a certain subject.

One of the teachers' organizations in particular—the Brooklyn Teachers' Association—arranges for special courses for teachers at very low rates, these courses to be given at central points in any one of the five boroughs. The courses cover all branches of cultural and professional education and include such recreation activities as swimming, dancing, photography, and dramatic art.

Leaves of Absence

In addition, the Board of Education has adopted the policy of granting to a limited number of teachers each year sabbatical leaves of absence for study, rest, travel or restoration of health. The teacher granted such a leave may receive for one term the difference between her regular salary and a substitute's pay for that term.

A by-law passed in January, 1924, provides that sabbatical leaves shall be granted to not more than fifty members of the teaching and supervising staff in high school and training schools, and to not more than one hundred in other day schools. However, the requests for leaves were so numerous that both in 1925-26 and 1926-27, the Board extended permission to more than three hundred teachers to be absent on leave. A teacher must have been in the system at least ten years before she may be granted a sabbatical leave. In recommending the granting of leaves, consideration is given, by a committee consisting of the associate superintendent in charge and two members of the Board of Education, to the teacher's record and length of service, and to the needs of the school system.

Leaves of absence for study or for restoration of health without pay may be obtained for one year or less by application to the Board of Superintendents.

Absence of a teacher from regular duty may be excused by the Local School Board of the district with no deduction in salary, subject to the approval of the Board of Superintendents, for any of three reasons,—illness, death in the teacher's immediate family, or required attendance in court. Each teacher is allowed three days for visiting other schools if her principal so desires.

Maternity leaves may be granted without pay by the Board of Superintendents. Any married woman member of the teaching staff, as soon as she is aware of her pregnancy, must notify the Superintendent of Schools and must forthwith apply for and accept leave of absence for two years. Between 600 and 700 teachers are now absent from the city's school staff on maternity leave. Three hundred and ninety-nine such leaves were granted in the year 1925-26.

Retirement System

New York City, through the Teachers' Retirement System, materially helps its teachers to prepare for disability or old age. The Teachers' Retirement System is really a compulsory thrift system. As soon as a teacher in the city schools has received her permanent license at the end of three years of approved service, she is automatically enlisted in the system and monthly deductions are made from her salary on the basis of the salary she receives and her years of service. The usual deduction is three percent of the salary for those who were in the service in 1917, but a teacher entering the service since that date must pay such percentage of her salary as shall be computed to be sufficient to pay one-half the cost of a retirement allowance of half average salary after thirty-five years of service or on the attainment of sixty-five years. For every annuity provided from contributions thus made by the teacher to the retirement fund, the city pays a like premium. By the time the teacher, then, has taught thirty-five years or has reached the age of retirement, sixty-five, she is entitled to a retirement allowance amounting to approximately one-half of the average salary she has received for her last five years of service. Retirement is mandatory at the age of seventy.

If, in the meantime, the teacher leaves the service for any reason, the sum of her contributions is returned to her with interest compounded at four percent. If she is disabled at the end of ten years of service in the city, she is entitled to receive a minimum of about twenty-five percent of her average salary for the last five years, and this disability allowance increases with her years of service up to approximately forty-five percent of her average salary for the previous five years. For a disability allowance the teacher must have had ten years in the city's service. For her service retirement allowance she may claim service elsewhere prior to becoming a member of the Teachers' Retirement System.

In case of the death of a teacher eligible for a service retirement allowance, her beneficiary is entitled to a sum amounting to one-half of the teacher's salary for the year preceding her death, in addition to the return of her contributions with interest. If death comes before a teacher is eligible, her beneficiary is entitled only to the sum of accumulated deductions from her salary with interest.

The foregoing is a very brief and sketchy account of the retirement system. There are many ramifications of that system into which it will be unnecessary to go here. The present system was established by an amendment to the city charter in 1917 to replace the old system which had proved to be on an unsound basis.* It was the first system in the country for municipal employees which called for the creation of reserves to pay benefits promised by the city as well as those provided by employees.

Directing the operation of the Teachers' Retirement System is a board of seven members composed of the President of the Board of Education, the City Comptroller, two members appointed by the Mayor, one of whom must be a member of the Board of Education, and three members elected by the contributors. This board elects its

---

*At the time of the 1917 amendment, in order to take care of teachers already in service, careful adjustments had to be made. The system as outlined above is that for new entrants in the service after 1917. The city has, in the case of teachers in service in 1917, made contributions greater than those made by the contributors in order to equalize allowances.

chairman and a secretary, appoints an actuary and necessary medical and clerical help, fixing their compensation subject to the approval of the Board of Estimate. The Board possesses the powers and privileges of a corporation to dispense the teachers' retirement funds. The Comptroller, who is custodian of the fund, makes payments on warrants signed by the chairman of the Board and countersigned by the secretary.

A medical board of three members examines all applicants for disability allowances. This board is made up of one physician appointed by contributing members of the retirement board, one physician appointed by the other members and one expert in women's and nervous diseases selected by the board as a whole. Teachers receiving a disability allowance must submit to medical examination yearly.

VII. ADMINISTERING THE SCHOOLS

I. OVERHEAD CONTROL OF EDUCATION

How the State Controls the Schools

THE State, first of all, is responsible for the schools. According to Article 9, Section 1, of the State Constitution, "The Legislature shall provide for the maintenance and support of a system of free common schools, wherein all the children of this State may be educated."

The Legislature

In compliance with this constitutional mandate, the Legislature has established by law certain minimum standards of education which must everywhere be met, and has provided state financial aid to enable communities to meet them. It has also created, for administrative purposes, a State Department of Education to supervise and direct the work of education in the state as a whole, and has defined the character and the powers of the various local school boards, which act as the agents of the State in their respective cities or school districts.

The Board of Regents

The State Department of Education is administered by a Board of Regents, appointed by the Legislature. This Board in turn selects the Commissioner of Education, who is the chief executive officer of the State school system and sees that all statutes, and all rules and regulations of the Board of Regents designed to carry out these statutes are duly enforced. The Regents are elected, one each year, by the Legislature, on joint ballot of the two houses, and there must be at least one Regent from each judicial district of the State. At the present time there are twelve Regents, each of whom serves for twelve years.

The Board of Regents is, in effect, the legislative body of the educational department of the State. Its jurisdiction is not confined, however, merely to the public school systems of the State. In addition to determining State public school policies within the statutes and holding local school authorities responsible for their official acts, the Regents act as the board of directors for the University of the State of New York.

This University is, of course, not a university in the usual sense of that term, with an institutional plant and a corps of teachers and students under its immediate direction. It is, rather, a corporate body endowed with legislative powers to encourage and promote education, to visit and inspect educational institutions and departments and to administer such property and funds as the State may appropriate or the University may hold in trust or otherwise. As a university board, the Regents may confer honorary degrees, or conduct examinations to confer degrees, diplomas or certificates. It establishes standards for graduation and college entrance for pupils in the public secondary schools. It fixes standards for evaluating diplomas or certificates issued by institutions of other states or foreign countries, which may be presented for entrance to schools, colleges or professions in the State. It has no control, however, over religious schools or theological institutions. In addition, it may charter any university, college, academy, library, museum, or other institution or association for the promotion of science, literature, art or education. It also supervises entrance regulations and licensing in such professions as medicine, dentistry, pharmacy, and optometry, and the certification of nurses, expert accountants, architects, etc., and appraises the diplomas issued by other states in these fields. It incorporates all correspondence schools, administers state scholarships, and has just recently been assigned the task of censoring motion pictures, which was formerly cared for by an independent commission created by the Legislature. The annual budget of the State Department, including the State normal schools and such other educational institutions as are under its direct control, is around $60,000,000.

From this brief sketch it may be seen that the State of New York has made a unique effort to coördinate and centralize its various educational functions and responsibilities, including that of publicly supported education, with which this story is particularly concerned.

The State Commissioner of Education

As has been indicated, to carry out these policies and to enforce its regulations, the Board of Regents appoints the Commissioner and such assistant commissioners and staff members as he and they may deem necessary. Exclusive of the State normal school faculties, the administrative staff of the State Department includes more than 750 persons. The Commissioner's functions fall into two main divisions: (1) administrative, subject to the direction of the Board of Regents; and (2) judicial, conferred separately upon him by law.

In his administrative capacity, as the chief executive officer of the State Department of Education, the Commissioner has power to enforce all the educational laws of the State, to execute all educational policies and regulations determined upon by the Regents, and in doing so to exercise general supervision over all schools and educational departments of the State and to investigate and examine them at his discretion.

In his judicial capacity, he acts as a supreme justice for educational matters in the State. He can hear and determine appeals or petitions from any one inside or outside the school system who believes himself to be aggrieved by acts occurring in the administration of the schools in any district in the State. He can annul upon cause shown to his satisfaction any certificate of qualification to a teacher. He can order the removal from office of any employee illegally appointed and remove from office any school officer who wilfully or through neglect of duty violates any law or regulation of the Regents or the Commissioner. He can also withhold public money of the State from any district or city which willfully disobeys or neglects to enforce any provision of the law or any regulation of the Regents.

Because of these broad administrative and judicial powers, it may be seen that the Commissioner is in an unusual position to be a powerful agent in determining school policies, in upholding high standards and in righting wrongs and determining controversies in any part of the State. The history of his office shows countless instances of the beneficial exercise of these prerogatives.

How the City Controls the Schools

As has already been indicated, the Legislature has set up local boards of education to care for the immediate

BOARD OF EDUCATION

administration of public schools. In most cities of the State these boards of education are elected by the people. In New York City and most of the larger cities, however, boards are appointed. In New York City the Board of Education comprises seven members, one of whom is appointed on May 1 each year by the Mayor to serve for a period of seven years. At the present time, two of these members must be from Manhattan, two from Brooklyn and one from each of the other three boroughs.

All of these local boards of education have very broad powers conferred upon them by the Legislature and most of them raise the money necessary to support their schools from local taxes which they themselves levy within certain statutory limits. In New York City, however, while the Board of Education has the same broad general educational powers as do other boards in the State, on the financial side it is dependent for its funds upon appropriations from the City Board of Estimate and Apportionment. As will be pointed out later, it must submit an annual budget to the City authorities, only part of which is guaranteed and upon which it can count. As a result, many of the educational policies in New York City are actually determined by the City authorities rather than by the Board of Education, because nothing can be undertaken unless funds are provided for maintenance.

Four Official Bodies Participate

So far as New York City is concerned, it is thus evident that four official bodies participate in determining the character of education offered.

In the first place, the Legislature passes laws specifically determining such matters as the powers and duties of the

Board of Education and other school officials, teachers' salaries, methods of selecting members of the professional staff, the establishment of continuation schools, the legal requirements for attendance, etc.

In the second place, the State Department of Education can amplify these statutes by rules and regulations respecting them, as it has done in the case of continuation schools and vocational education. The Commissioner, also, can intervene if he believes the law is not being properly enforced and can also hear and determine complaints in respect to the way the City is carrying out the statutes and, if necessary, withhold state appropriations until regulations of the State Department are properly carried out.

In the third place, the Board of Education sets up its own by-laws and appoints the administrative officers and subordinate members of the staff that are essential to carry out these laws and to maintain the standards indicated by the statutes and regulations of the State Department. It may, furthermore, consider these standards as mere minimum requirements and go as far as it wishes beyond them in providing local school facilities.

In this latter connection, however, the Board of Education runs up against the fourth factor in the control of schools, the financial authorities of the City—the Board of Estimate and Apportionment primarily—who can practically nullify anything which the Board of Education may want to do, provided the law does not make it mandatory. In fact, it will be seen later on that even the Board of Aldermen and the Mayor, through the power of veto, can take a share in shaping the policies of the Board of Education.

This distribution of authority and the power of the City financial authorities to veto practically anything which is not made mandatory explains the tendency in New York City to have as many policies as possible enacted into law by the Legislature. Particularly has this been true in the creation of certain types of education and in prescribing salary schedules and the retirement system.

The Board of Education

Turning now to the Board of Education of New York City specifically, its powers, subject to the foregoing limitations, may be briefly summarized as follows:

1. It can create, abolish, maintain or consolidate any positions, divisions, boards or bureaus that it may deem necessary for the administration of its work.

2. Subject to legal requirements as to nomination, hereafter noted, it can appoint superintendents, supervisors, teachers and such other professional and business employees as it may deem necessary in its work.

3. Unless the law specifically defines the duties of these employees, as it does, for example, in the case of the Superintendent of Schools and the Board of Examiners, the Board of Education can definitely determine exactly what each employee shall do.

4. The Board of Education has the custody and control of all school property and can prescribe rules and regulations for its use and preservation.

5. It selects sites and authorizes the erection of buildings, purchases and furnishes books and furniture, and provides all the apparatus, equipment, and supplies necessary to carry on its program.

6. It can establish and maintain libraries, organize public lecture courses, and equip playgrounds, recreation

centers, social centers, etc., within the limits of the funds it can obtain from the Board of Estimate.

In addition to the foregoing powers, which it can perform entirely on its own initiative, it performs certain functions on the recommendation of the Board of Superintendents which it appoints in accordance with the statutes and which comprises the superintendent and eight associate superintendents. These latter functions include such matters as the authorization of courses of study, the adoption of textbooks and the appointment of all members of the teaching and supervisory staff except the superintendent of schools and associate superintendents whom it appoints entirely on its own initiative. It should be noted here that it also appoints members of the Board of Examiners without recommendation by the Board of Superintendents, only in this case its choice is confined to an eligible list prepared by the Municipal Civil Service Commission.

The Board must also use municipal civil service lists for all of its non-professional employees such as draftsmen, janitors, stenographers, clerks, etc., unless those positions are specifically exempted by statutes or by action of the Municipal Civil Service Commission.

By this broad control over appointments and educational and business policies the Board of Education is thus empowered to make final decisions within the limits above described as to the conduct of the public schools in New York City. Not only can it define policies but it may cause such reports and accounts to be kept as it may require, and it may institute such inquiries or investigations as it shall deem necessary in formulating such policies and programs or in administering the schools of New York City.

How the Board of Education Operates

Without elaborating in detail on how the Board goes about its work, it is interesting to note that, like many boards of directors, the Board of Education does the larger part of its work through committees. At the present time the Board has the following committees: finance and budget; buildings and sites; day schools; evening schools; departmental organization; special schools; law; continuation schools and speech improvement; physical training; supplies; care of buildings; Bureau of Attendance; lectures; and local school boards.

After these special committees have passed upon purely routine matters, the Board itself usually accepts their recommendations without comment. Matters of policy are discussed more thoroughly in the Board as a whole and, on mooted questions, the Board sometimes calls public hearings so that interested citizens may have an opportunity to express their views.

The officers of the Board of Education are the president and vice-president, who act as presiding officers and naturally have a commanding position in the conduct of the Board's affairs. The details connected with the Board's actions and deliberations are cared for by its secretary who is an intermediary between the Board and the schools.

The Secretary of the Board of Education

As soon as possible after each meeting of the Board of Education, the secretary notifies the officers of the Board of all action taken by the Board affecting the respective departments. He notifies all members of the teaching and supervising staff, and other employees of the Board, of appointments, promotions and transfers authorized. He makes requisition upon the Civil Service Commission for the names of persons to be appointed to positions which are subject to its rules and regulations, and he notifies this Commission of the appointment, promotion, transfer, resignation or removal of such employees.

On behalf of the Board of Education, he prepares and executes all contracts after they have been awarded and secures the execution of such contracts by the contractors. On behalf of the Board, he also prepares and executes all leases which have been duly authorized and approved according to law. He notifies the Board of Education of the expiration of the terms of office of its officers and employees and has charge of the books, papers and documents of the Board of Education and the custody of the corporate seal.

For the accomplishment of these and various other duties that the Board of Education and its president may assign to him, the secretary is allowed a staff of thirty-two persons, including two assistant secretaries.

Local School Boards

In a city so huge as New York it would be unfitting for the citizens of a school district not to have a closer contact with the control of the schools than that afforded by representatives of each borough appointed by the Mayor to serve on the Board of Education. This closer contact in New York City is afforded by the local district school boards, which, indeed, have very little actual power but which serve to give the citizens a chance to voice the needs of their districts.

The larger school district comprised by New York City is divided for school administration purposes into fifty-four smaller districts. A local school board is made up of

BOARD OF EDUCATION

five members selected from the residents of the local district by the Borough President, who is himself an elected official. In addition the district superintendent is required to attend all meetings although he has no vote and is not eligible to office; and one member of the Board of Education assigned to the district is a member of the Board with a vote, but not eligible to office.

It is the duty of the local school board to inspect all the schools in the district at least once each quarter and report to the Board of Education any matter requiring official action. The members are particularly charged with the inspection of the physical condition of buildings, of seeing that the children of the district are suitably housed and that the buildings are kept in order; they are asked to make recommendations to the Board of Education regarding new buildings needed and to suggest possible new sites. These matters, too, are part of the job of the district superintendent and since he is in closer daily touch with the schools than the local board members he is in a position to suggest to the local school board any conditions of overcrowding or poor or unsafe or ill-kept school buildings that need investigation and attention.

One other important function of the local board is that of investigating any complaints made against a principal, teacher or other school employee in the district and reporting to the Board of Education thereon. In case the Superintendent of Schools sees fit to prefer charges against any such school employee for violation of a school regulation the local board has a hearing on those charges and makes a report to the Board of Education. The Board of Education may then reject, confirm or modify their recommendation. The local board may also excuse teachers' absence either with or without pay, subject to the approval of the Board of Superintendents.

As can readily be seen most of the powers delegated to local boards are advisory and investigatory; nevertheless a determined local board of enterprising and interested citizens have a very influential medium through which to make their voices heard and to bring needed changes to the attention of higher powers.

II. INTERNAL ADMINISTRATION OF THE SCHOOLS

JUST as the Board of Regents, acting for the State, administers its work through the Commissioner of Education as its chief executive officer, so each of the local school boards of education in the school districts throughout the State administers its work through a superintendent of schools as its chief executive officer. So, too, just as the law confers certain definite powers upon the Commissioner of Education, it also confers very definite powers upon each of these local superintendents.

In every school district in the State except New York City, which itself constitutes a school district, these powers are exercised by the superintendent as an individual. In New York City, however, most of these powers are exercised by the Board of Superintendents, comprising the Superintendent of Schools, as chairman, and his eight associate superintendents, all of whom, as has been indicated, are appointed by the Board of Education for a six-year term. It thus happens that, whereas elsewhere in the State all the fundamental professional policies are determined by the superintendent, as an individual, with the approval of his board of education, in New York City most of these policies are decided by vote of the Board of Superintendents. It is thus possible for a majority of the eight associate superintendents to outvote the superintendent and to adopt measures which might not be proposed or enforced if he were fully in charge, as are superintendents elsewhere in the State and in the nation at large.

The Board of Superintendents

The significance of this arrangement is indicated by the following list of important powers and duties which are conferred upon the Board of Superintendents rather than upon the Superintendent alone:

1. To prepare courses of study and recommend suitable textbooks, library books and educational supplies; to prepare syllabi in subjects of the curriculum.

2. To recommend kinds and grades of licenses to be required and also qualifications for each kind and grade.

3. To recommend new school buildings and building sites.

4. To recommend all appointments to teaching and supervisory positions except superintendent, associate superintendents and examiners.

5. To make recommendations upon the quality of work of teachers in the three-year probationary period.

6. To recommend changes in the kind or grade of schools.

7. To make regulations for the administration, transfer and promotion of pupils.

The City Superintendent of Schools

This leaves to the Superintendent of Schools only such individual powers and duties as the following:

1. To enforce laws and regulations of the Board of Education relating to the management of schools and other educational, social, and recreational activities under the direction of the Board of Education.

2. To supervise all school employees, report any violations of law, and make temporary suspensions pending

action by the Board of Education of employees suspected of violations.

3. To issue teachers' licenses upon the recommendation of the Board of Examiners.

4. To assign the district superintendents to supervision of certain divisions.

5. To visit or cause all schools to be visited and examined annually.

6. To fix office hours for associate and district superintendents and make a manual of regulations for all other employees.

7. To report to the retirement board the names of teachers eligible for any allotment of funds from it.

In addition to serving as members of the Board of Superintendents, however, the associate superintendents are also assigned certain administrative duties under the immediate direction of the Superintendent of Schools. The City is divided into broad school divisions for each one of which an associate is responsible. The associates also supervise and administer certain bureaus and departments and report to the Superintendent and the Board of Education at the close of each school year on the conditions in their respective divisions and upon the special activities under their supervision.

The District Superintendents

The Board of Superintendents thus comprises the central organizing and supervising force of the school system. Under its direction the schools are administered by a network of subordinate officials.

In the first place come the district superintendents. The city is divided into fifty-four school districts as has been pointed out previously, for each of which there is a local school board. To every two of these districts a district superintendent, appointed for permanent tenure by the Board of Education on the nomination of the Board of Superintendents, is assigned. These assignments vary in size and complexity, but each one of them is larger in school registration than most of the school systems elsewhere in the State or in the country.

Twenty-seven of the district superintendents are thus assigned to districts. They supervise and inspect all the schools in their respective districts except the junior high schools, continuation schools, high schools and training schools. Two district superintendents are assigned to high schools, one to continuation schools, one to junior high schools, and one to training schools, making thirty-two district superintendents in all.

THE DIRECTORS AND INSPECTORS OF SPECIAL BRANCHES

In addition to the foregoing supervision of instruction and school management on a district basis, the various special branches and special functions are also supervised from headquarters for the school system as a whole. Among the more important of the special directorships are directors of kindergartens, music, art and drawing, art in high schools, sewing, speech improvement, extension activities, physical training, evening and continuation schools, vocational education, lectures, modern languages in high schools and foreign languages in junior high schools. Other officials who are in effect directors of special branches are called inspectors. There are inspectors of ungraded classes, of playgrounds and recreation centers, of classes for the blind, of industrial and placement work for handicapped children and of public school athletics. In addition to these are assistant directors with special functions, such as the assistant director of visual instruction in the Bureau of Lectures, the assistant director of manual training, assistant directors of educational hygiene in the physical training department, etc. A director is also specially assigned to high school organization. There is an officer especially assigned to the supervision of civics in high school, another to school gardens. There is, too, a manager of school lunches. All of these are branches or divisions requiring expert and special knowledge.

These directors and inspectors are appointed for permanent tenure by the Board of Education on recommendation of the Board of Superintendents and serve as advisers to the Board of Superintendents, the district superintendents and principals. They give instruction in their several branches to special teachers and regular class teachers and examine and make reports upon the work as it is taught in the schools.

THE PRINCIPALS

Immediately in charge of each school is the principal. Elementary, junior high school, continuation and trade school principals are appointed by the Board of Education on recommendation of the Board of Superintendents from eligible lists based on ratings received in competitive examinations. One or more administrative assistants are allowed according to the size of the schools. These assistant principals are also appointed from eligible lists.

Requests from a school principal are always given weight in assigning teachers and assistants, of course. Assignment, transfer and promotion of teachers is the special charge of one of the associate superintendents. Candidates for teaching and supervising positions usually limit the appointment they will accept to certain boroughs or parts of boroughs, and the office of the associate superintendent makes an effort to adjust assignments and transfers in accordance with the preference of both teachers and principals.

The principal is directly responsible both for the educational work in his school and for the physical condition of his building. He inspects and examines class work, and reports upon the work of teachers. He holds teachers' conferences, and conducts or has conducted model lessons. He makes requisition to the district superintendent for textbooks, apparatus and supplies. He supervises the custodian and notifies the local school board of injuries to the buildings and needed repairs. He makes out the payroll for the teaching and supervisory staff of the school and files it in the auditor's office.

High school and training school principals are selected by the Board of Education on the recommendations of the Board of Superintendents without reference to the Board of Examiners; high school assistants to principals, however, are selected from eligible lists. Their powers as to courses of study, school management and organization are less restricted than those of principals in the lower schools; they are left rather more room to experiment and to work out their own ideas and plans of organization.

Special Boards and Bureaus

In addition to the regular staff of the educational system directly in contact with administration of certain schools and departments, there are a number of advisory boards which should receive mention here.

The Bureau of Reference, Research and Statistics

In the first place, there is the Bureau of Reference, Research and Statistics which performs an invaluable service to the school system by conducting scientific experimental work. It compiles data on various educational projects and investigates all matters of education referred to it by the Board of Superintendents or the Board of Education. The Bureau is, as its name suggests, first of all, a bureau to make research into matters of vital importance in schools and to make available clarifying data on those matters to the teaching and supervisory staff and to the general public. Its second duty, as has been explained in some detail,* is to carry on, at the request of the Board of Superintendents, certain specific experiments with a view to determining changes in educational policy and practice.

Besides the director and assistant director, the Bureau has now assigned to it four administrative officers and has a clerical staff of thirty-nine. In addition, the Superintendent assigns from time to time members of the supervisory staff to help with some specific work. In 1926-27, the Bureau operated on a budget of $114,035.

A third duty of this Bureau is the publication of reports and the making of statistical charts authorized or approved by the Board of Superintendents and by the Board of Education. The Bureau itself is required to make annual report of its activities to the Board of Education.

---
*See page 13.

The Advisory Board on Industrial Education

The Bureau of Reference, Research and Statistics is an integral part of the school system conducted by a salaried staff. The Advisory Board on Industrial Education is, as its name indicates, a board without salary and without administrative powers.

With the growing demand for industrial education in the schools, with the federal Smith-Hughes law requiring the teaching of vocational courses and with the state continuation school laws providing for the continuance of education for employed children between the ages of fourteen and eighteen, the schools, already experimenting with industrial education, were forced to greatly extend their activities. To aid the educational officials in this work it was provided that an advisory board of five members representing local trades, industries and occupations be appointed by the Board of Education to counsel and advise school directors in all matters relating to training in public schools for gainful occupations. The powers of this Board are advisory only, but its establishment has given invaluable opportunity to representatives of the various trades to coöperate with school men in suggesting or outlining courses and in suggesting needed equipment.

Partly through the efforts of this advisory board, partly through other interested labor leaders and employers, apprentices in many trades are now required to continue in evening or continuation schools for two, three or four years of their apprenticeship. Incidentally, these same labor leaders or representatives of employers are often instrumental in getting for the schools certain expensive equipment which they deem necessary to approximate in the school shops the working conditions in the actual shops where the children will be employed. Again, in the planning and equipment of evening and continuation school courses, the coöperation between the schools and the trades has brought about a superior type of trade work in the schools.

The Teachers' Council

In order that the principals and teachers might have a medium through which to make themselves heard by the Board of Superintendents and Board of Education, the Board of Education in 1913 approved a plan to establish a Teachers' Council. The functions of this council are two-fold:

1. To furnish information and opinions of the teaching staff upon questions submitted by the Board of Education or the Board of Superintendents.
2. To make recommendations concerning any problems affecting the welfare of schools or the teaching staff.

The Council is made up of representatives of voluntary teachers' organizations recognized by the Board of Education. Representation is proportioned among these organizations by the Council's by-laws. Members are elected yearly, as are the officers of the Council.

While the Superintendent and members of the Board of Education are in no way constrained to accept the recommendations of the Council, yet the Council aims, like the local school boards, to do two things: (1) to present to the central boards in charge of schools the viewpoint of persons more directly in contact with schools and school children; and (2) to give the teachers a medium through which to express their ideas about needed changes in the schools.

The following list of the Associations whose representatives take part in the deliberations of the Council will serve to indicate the numerous and varied activities of the New York City schools:

Association Teachers of Shopwork of the City of New York.
Association of Assistant Directors of Physical Training, Educational Hygiene, Music and Manual Training of New York City.
Association of Assistants to Principal of New York City.
Association of Male First Assistants in High Schools of New York City.
Association of Model Teachers of the City of New York.
Association of Public School Teachers of Crippled Children in the City of New York.
Association of Public School Teachers of the Deaf.
Association of Supervisory Teachers of Domestic Art.
Association of Supervisory Teachers of Drawing of Greater New York.
Association of Teachers in Charge of Elementary Schools.
Association of Women High School Teachers.
Association of Women Principals of Public Schools in the City of New York.
Association of Workers among Delinquent Children.
Brooklyn Principals' Council.
Brooklyn Teachers' Association.
Brooklyn Women Principals' Association.
Class Teachers' Organization of Brooklyn.
Council of Attendance Officers.
Continuation School Teachers' Association.
Critic Teachers' Association.
Evening High School Teachers' Association.
Heads of Department Association of the Borough of Brooklyn.
High School Clerical Assistants' Association.
High School Principals' Association.
High School Teachers' Association of New York City.

Home Economics Association of Teachers of Elementary Schools of New York City.
Industrial Art Teachers' Association of Evening High Schools of New York City.
Interborough Association of Women Teachers.
Male Principals' Association of Borough of Queens.
Men Principals' Association, Manhattan and the Bronx.
Music Teachers' Association.
New York Association of Biology Teachers.
New York Association of High School Teachers of German.
New York City Association of Men Principals.
New York City Association of Teachers of English.
New York City Association of Women Principals.
New York City Teachers' Association.
New York High School Librarians' Association.
New York Vocational Teachers' Council.
Physical Training Teachers' Association of Greater New York.
Professional Elementary Teachers' Association.
Public School Kindergarten Association of New York City.
Recreation Centre Teachers' Association.
Seventh, Eighth and Ninth Year Women Teachers' Association of the City of New York.
Speech Improvement Teachers' Association of the City of New York.
Staten Island Teachers' Association.
Staten Island Women Teachers' Club.
Teachers' Association of the Borough of Queens.
Teachers' Interests' Organization.
Ungraded Teachers' Association of New York.
Vacation High School Teachers' Association.

In addition to these there are several other organizations, as, for example, the Teachers' Union, whose activities influence the status of the teachers and the schools. No list of organizations of New York teachers would be complete without mention of the New York Society for the Experimental Study of Education. The purpose of this organization is succinctly stated in its title. It enrolls about 1,500 teachers and has functioned for ten years. The teachers meet in groups—about thirty-five sections each studying some particular phase of elementary or secondary education—once a month from October to May, usually in Washington Irving High School. They compare notes on experiments conducted in various schools and classes of the city, with a view, not only to disseminating the experience gained from those experiments, but also to encouraging and inspiring further study and experiment on the part of teachers and supervisors.

III. BUSINESS ADMINISTRATION OF THE SCHOOLS

Making the Annual Budget and Securing Funds

THE main sources of school moneys are three: (1) city appropriations raised by tax levy, (2) money borrowed through the sale of bonds, and (3) state grants.

After taking into consideration the amounts estimated as available from State sources, appropriations by the city for recurring needs of the schools are provided out of the annual tax on real and personal property. The rate of tax depends, of course, upon the amount of money allowed in the budget for all the city departments by the Board of Estimate and the Board of Aldermen.

How School Moneys are Apportioned

All school moneys for annual operating expenses are apportioned in two funds. In the general fund are included the salaries of the superintendent, associate superintendents, district superintendents, director and assistant director of the Division of Reference, Research and Statistics, members of the Board of Examiners, attendance officers, lecturers and all members of the supervising and teaching staff. In the special fund are included all school moneys for annual operating expenses other than the general fund.

How the Budget is Made by the School Authorities

The compilation of an educational tax budget which involves more than one hundred million dollars, the details of which come from many persons and sources, is naturally a task requiring several months and many hours of labor. The chronological story of budget-making runs as follows: First, the Superintendent of Schools in the early spring directs all executive officials, associate superintendents, directors of special branches, inspectors, etc., to prepare estimates of the sums they will need for the next year. All estimates for teaching service for the ensuing calendar year are based upon register, number of classes, number of employees in service, etc., as of the date March 31st of the current year plus allowances for increased register, and improvements or extensions of service.

The estimates must be in the Superintendent's hands by May 10th or 15th so that he may hold hearings in which the superintendents, directors and department heads may explain the need of increased appropriations or of any changes they desire to make in the budget. The Superintendent then sends the estimates that he has received together with whatever recommendations he wishes to make concerning them to the Board of Education's committee on finance and budget.

This committee is made up of three members of the Board. They go over every item of the budget estimates and the Superintendent's recommendations and call hearings on the estimates from every department. These hearings usually require from thirty to forty-five whole days and are attended by the Superintendent of Schools, the Auditor, and the Director of Reference, Research and Statistics, or their representatives, and by the head of the department or activity whose budget is under consideration, as well as by representatives of the Board of Estimate and of the Commissioner of Accounts on behalf of the City government.

At these hearings the superintendents, directors and department heads again have a chance to explain their requests, to show the need for any improvements or extensions of service for which they have asked, and to answer any questions concerning their estimates. The estimates, themselves, of course, reflect school policies as formulated by the Board of Superintendents and carried by them back to those more directly in touch with administration—the directors and district superintendents.

Before the tentative budget estimate is presented for action, public hearings are held by the committee on finance and budget, and the Board of Education sits as a committee of the whole for several days to consider the budget estimate, so that when it is presented to them as a board it is usually passed immediately without comment. This budget estimate must then be filed with the Board of Estimate by September 1st.

How the Budget is Passed upon by the City

The Board of Estimate considers the items and calls hearings when requested until October 10th when its tentative budget covering all departments of the city government must be published. From October 10th to 20th any additions may be made to items in that tentative budget; after October 20th, the Board of Estimate may still subtract from the proposed items but may not add to them.

On October 31st, the budget passes out of the hands of the Board of Estimate to the Board of Aldermen which may only cut the figures, not add to them. Moreover, the Mayor who has sat with the Board of Estimate through its deliberation on the budget has the veto power over any subtractions the Aldermen may make. The budget finally is passed by the Board of Aldermen and prior to December 25th is certified by the Mayor, the Comptroller and the City Clerk, and the appropriations are then legally in effect.

The budget estimate, as prepared by the Auditor of the Board of Education, is of necessity a rather awesome collection of figures. Increases or decreases are made ascertainable by tables showing costs on the March 31st previous, on December 31st to follow, and in the case of salaries, aggregate annual rates for the ensuing year.

The compilation of the City budget takes note of course of the sums which will come to the City from the State, and through the State, from the Federal Educational Bureau. The state sums are apportioned in accordance with state law and must be used for teachers' salaries.

How the State Aids in Supporting the Schools

The estimate of State and Federal aid to the City for use during 1926–27 totalled $23,806,954.52. This sum included quotas for vocational schools, courses in Americanization, physical training and handicapped classes.

The largest one item in the State appropriation is the teacher quota—an appropriation of $750 per teacher.

The passage this year of the Dick-Rice bill based on the findings of the Governor's Commission on School Finance carrying with it an appropriation of the $16,500,000, will allow to New York City approximately $10,600,000 additional state aid in 1927–28 and gradually increasing sums for the next three years.

How Funds are Borrowed for School Construction

Now the budget estimate of moneys needed from the city exchequer to run the schools is a request merely for recurring annual expenses of conducting the school system. It does not include capital outlay for new buildings or more lands for use of the educational department. When the city of New York wishes to buy land or to erect buildings, it is permitted by law to borrow money through the sale of bonds, the money to be repaid to the bondholders over a long period of time. In this way the taxpayers of today will not be made to stand the whole cost of buildings that may serve several generations of school children.

When the Board of Education wishes to borrow money thus for lands or buildings it presents to the Board of Estimate, usually in January, the corporate stock budget. This budget is in effect the Board's building program for the year. It lists item by item, location, cost and size of sites to be acquired and of buildings to be erected and repairs to be made. The process by which the educational authorities decide upon a building program is as intricate as that of making the annual budget estimate of operating expenses.

First, the Superintendent of Schools issues instructions to prepare the corporate stock budget—that is, the building program for the year. The Superintendent then requests the preparation of data by the associate superintendent in charge of buildings.

This associate superintendent has the building problems as his sole assignment. It is his function to maintain a survey of the school population, to note and take account in his building program of shifts of population and of changing conditions in certain districts that will necessitate different types of sites and building plans. He must take account of the need of vocational schools in this district, of more continuation schools in that, of an ever increasing number of children flocking to the high schools in still a third district.

Such data will then be considered by the Board of Superintendents who will make recommendations to the Board of Education's Committee on Buildings and Sites. Next the proposed program will go to the Board of Education as a whole for approval.

Following that approval, the secretary will forward the budget to the Board of Estimate and Apportionment where it will be considered first by the committee on finance and budget. That committee will have the plans and specifications gone over by its engineers and will then make recommendation back to the Board of Estimate. The Board of Estimate will finally act upon its committee's recommendation and notify the Board of Education.

That is for the program as a whole. The process of securing the erection of a particular building is described in the section on the work of the Bureau of Construction and Maintenance.

The Board of Estimate may do one or two things when the corporate stock budget is presented to it. It sometimes passes a resolution to allow the sum asked by the Board of Education in making up its corporate stock budget for the whole city; or it may choose to pass upon each item of the school program as it is presented during the year, in accordance with the process described above.

The Comptroller of the City is authorized to sell bonds for school and other purposes by the Board of Estimate and Apportionment. The City may not at any time, however, have a bonded indebtedness for all municipal purposes of more than ten percent of the assessed valuation of its real and personal property liable to taxation. The City is em-

BUSINESS ADMINISTRATION

powered in case of an emergency need to issue special revenue bonds, but since the proceeds of the sale of these bonds is for current purposes, they must be redeemed out of the taxes of the following year.

AUDITING ACCOUNTS

All the accounts of the Board of Education are administered by the Bureau of Finance which is headed by the Auditor. The personnel of this Bureau consists of 121 persons who handle annually about 90,000 claims for supplies, equipment, repairs, etc., and 13,000 payrolls for salaries, and carry on the business necessary to (1) the keeping of all formal funds, accounts and collateral records, (2) the compilation of financial statistics, and (3) the auditing of all claims involving the expenditure of moneys.

The moneys handled annually will be indicated by the following list applying to the year 1925:

Budget Accounts (Tax levy and State moneys, many subdivisions)	$100,722,207.28
State High School Trust Fund	51,300.13
State Trust Fund for Maintenance of Training Schools	58,237.14
State Trust Fund for School Libraries	29,719.87
Special Fund—Collections for School Lunches	76,992.05
Special Fund—Collections for Use of Auditoriums	5,313.22
Special Fund—Sale of Products of Manhattan Trade School	12,982.42
Fire Prevention Accounts	500,000.00
Accounts of the Employees' Retirement System	631,738.25
Accounts of Hunter College	1,055,056.17
Corporate Stock Accounts (Many subdivisions)	11,519,220.47
	$114,662,767.00

These are continuing accounts to which has been added at frequent but irregular intervals from 1918 to 1927 the sum of $185,177,800.00 for the acquisition of sites and the erection of buildings.

In addition to the above, the Bureau of Finance has supervision of the school savings banks; computes deductions from salaries, certifications as to average salary, etc., for the Teachers' Retirement Board; investigates and reports in matters of actual or threatened legal actions, collections from sureties on defaulted contracts, etc.; prepares financial resolutions for the Board of Education and prepares and publishes the annual financial and statistical report of the Board of Education.

Last, but not least, there is the work done by the Auditor and his staff, and other officials of the Board of Education, in preparing the annual budget already described in the preceding section.

Erecting Buildings

The Board of Education, facing the fact that circumstances had conspired to cause a serious school seating shortage, has been struggling for many years with the housing problem. Early in 1923 an intensive school building program was launched for the purpose of coping with the serious overcrowding in school buildings. This campaign was also intended to establish new standards in construction of buildings and so far as possible to apply these standards to the existing buildings wherever the maintenance work made it practicable to do so.

The Bureau of Construction and Maintenance

The conduct of this building work is in charge of the Bureau of Construction and Maintenance. Its work is divided into two main divisions,—the one carrying on the planning and supervision of new building construction work and the other, conducted by five deputy superintendents of school buildings, with a separate office located in each of the five boroughs of the city, in charge of maintenance and betterment of the existing school buildings.

After a building for a certain number of pupils for certain activities has been approved by the Board of Education, the architects of the building bureau confer frequently with members of the pedagogical staff so that the building will be complete in detail and constructed as economically as is consistent with the character, size and importance of the structure. Also, whenever new standards in the planning of buildings or in the arrangement of equipment are undertaken or old standards are reviewed and revised, conferences are conducted under the jurisdiction of the Board of Superintendents, at which are present several executives of the pedagogical staff, and a proper representation of the architectural staff.

Steps Required to Authorize a School Building

The process of erecting a school building from the time of deciding that it must be to the time of its completion is a long one. Once the corporate stock budget is made up, the process for authorizing and building a particular building is somewhat as follows:

1. Report of associate superintendent to the Board of Superintendents as to the requirements of any particular building—number of rooms, grades, etc.
2. Action by Board of Superintendents.
3. Report to the Board of Education. Consideration by committee on building and sites.
4. Approval by the Board of Education.
5. Copy forwarded by the secretary of the Board of Education to the Superintendent of School Buildings.
6. Obtaining of the building survey, and
7. Consideration by the Superintendent of School Buildings as to what plan would best meet the requirements.
8. Consultation with pedagogical staff.

9. Preparation of plans in the draughting-room.//
10. Submission of preliminary design to the Municipal Art Commission.
11. At completion of drawing, submission for final approval of the Municipal Art Commission.
12. Submission and approval of Bureau of Buildings in the borough in which the job is located.
13. If plumbing, gas-fitting and electric work are included, submission to the Department of Water Supply, Gas and Electricity.
14. Preparation and printing of specifications.
15. Submission to and approval by Board of Education.
16. Forwarding of notice of such approval of resolutions by the secretary of the Board to the Board of Estimate and Apportionment.
17. Reference to committee of the whole of the Board of Estimate and Apportionment.
18. Reference to the engineers of this committee.
19. Report back to the committee of the whole.
20. Action by this committee.
21. Action by Board of Estimate and Apportionment.
22. Notice to secretary of Board of Education.
23. Notice from secretary to the Superintendent of School Buildings.
24. Submission to the Corporation Counsel for approval of form of contract and advertisement.
25. Filing in the City Record and advertising for ten days.
26. Opening of bids by Superintendent of School Buildings.
27. Report to Board of Education.
28. Making of award.
29. Notification to the Comptroller for the approval of sureties.
30. Then return to Board of Education.
31. Surety bonds attached.
32. Contract signed.
33. To Auditor for recording.
34. Then its return to the Comptroller for his final approval.

35. Notice of which is received, and
36. Conveyed to the deputy superintendents of buildings.
37. Notice to the contractor to begin work.

Recent Progress in School Building

When it is considered that in spite of this complicated process more school buildings have been built in the last three and one-half years than in the next six largest cities of the country combined, some idea is gained of the magnitude of the building enterprise conducted by the Board, and the necessity for coördinating the work of its various departments. For, in that time, 145 new school buildings and additions have been completed and occupied by 211,296 pupils at an aggregate cost of $113,489,835, not including the cost of the sites on which the buildings have been located.

Problems Involved in School Construction

The school housing problems in this huge cosmopolitan center are greatly varied. To provide a new school building to accommodate 2,700 pupils in a congested section requires an entirely different plan and structure design than for a school for an equal number of pupils to be built in an outlying section.

Not alone has the architectural department of the Board of Education been occupied with overcoming the many practical difficulties, but it has also aimed to keep apace with the great strides made in the last decade in the architectual design of buildings. Undoubtedly the improvement made in school building designing has had its cheering influence on the occupants and has established a sentiment and attachment among the pupils for the school.

Operating Buildings

The Bureau of Plant Operation is responsible for the care of all buildings used by the Board of Education and for the repair and maintenance of all heating and ventilating plants and mechanical equipment used in those buildings. This means that the Bureau has in charge 750 buildings owned by the Board of Education and 134 more loaned or leased to the Board—884 in all. The 1926 budget of the Bureau amounted to $6,734,338.15.

Its functions divide the Bureau into two divisions, the custodial or housekeeping service and the heating and ventilating division.

Care of school buildings is provided for in two different ways:

1. The direct system plan—civil service—under which all the help required in the care of the school building is employed directly by the Board of Education.

2. The indirect system plan—contract—under which a flat allowance is made for the care of the school building which is paid to the custodian-engineer or custodian in equal monthly installments, out of which he pays the help he employs in the care of such school building. It is estimated there are about 3,200 persons employed under the indirect system.

The present superintendent of the Bureau recommends that all of the schools be brought under the second plan. Under both plans the employees must be chosen from eligible lists specially prepared by the Municipal Civil Service Commission and after a short probationary period, varying with the type of job, have practically permanent tenure, providing always, of course, that they continue to do the job properly.

The second or indirect plan has been installed in all but fourteen schools. The sum allotted to the contracting custodian is based upon certain standard calculations which, in turn, are based upon the building area, the paved area and the type of heating and ventilating plant in a building.

The inspection of buildings under both plans is in the hands of inspectors from the central office.

Qualifications of custodians and custodian engineers are carefully looked into by the Civil Service Commission which maintains a separate eligible list for school employees, and in addition, the custodian-engineers must have a license from the Police Department based upon statements of several engineers that they are qualified. Further insuring the competence of the custodians and the safety of the school plant annual tests of boilers in the school buildings are made by the Police Department.

Supplying the Schools

Upon the Bureau of Supplies devolves the task of supplying the schools with all the books, equipment, janitorial supplies, scientific supplies and apparatus, pianos and organs required by all the schools under the direction of the Board of Education, from the kindergartens to the training schools and including all the special classes and branches of educational work. This Bureau too furnishes transportation for pupils when necessary, provides film service for visual instruction, and apparatus and supplies for vacation schools and playgrounds.

To indicate the variety of activities carried on by the Bureau of Supplies a few distinctive items might be cited:

Allotment of school supplies to each school is based on the number and grade of pupils in the school. All the necessary books, supplies, and equipment for the children in the grades from kindergarten to 8B, including the materials required for instruction in sewing, drawing, kindergarten work, cooking, work-shop practice and for the classes for anæmic, tubercular, deaf, blind and crippled children, are furnished at approximately one penny per child per day.

All the supplies required by the high school pupils amount to a cost of about two and a half cents per child per day.

Supplies are furnished for the school lunches in thirty schools in the various boroughs. The cost is kept very low by advertising and purchasing supplies under contract or on competitive estimates.

The amount expended for the transportation of pupils is nearly $400,000 yearly. Of this amount $70,000 to $80,000 is for trolley and bus line tickets furnished to the pupils.

The delivery division of the Bureau receives supplies at four central depositories whence they are delivered to the schools at the proper time. But because of lack of space in these depositories many deliveries have to be made directly to schools.

Principals make their requisitions for supplies upon official printed lists. Approximately 100,000 requisitions are received by the Bureau yearly, 30,000 orders are issued, 45,000 bills passed and 1,000,000 contract items tabulated. The total amounts of funds expended under the jurisdiction of this Bureau is $5,500,000.

All coal is purchased under contract and on an analysis basis. When all the new schools now under construction are completed, an annual tonnage of from 190,000 to 200,000 tons will be needed to heat and ventilate the schools. Coal has also been provided to heat water for pools, showers, domestic science purposes, cleaning, etc.

The inspectors of fuel weigh every load of coal supplied to the buildings under the control of the Board of Education. They also measure all the wood furnished for kindling purposes for boilers, stoves, heaters, etc. A visual examination is made of all coal before accepting it; samples are taken and sent to the city laboratory for analysis, and payment for the coal is based on the results obtained.

Lumber for use in the shops is sent direct to the schools from five separate lumber yards. It is inspected, measured, checked and accounted for by inspectors assigned from the Bureau of Supplies. There are forty-nine different kinds and sizes of lumber.

Operating the garage and transportation equipment is also under the control of the Bureau of Supplies.

Increase in the Bureau's staff or in the facilities at its disposal has not been proportional to the growth of the school system in the last few years. Many new buildings have been opened and supplied by the Bureau with much the same staff as formerly.

The Bureau needs a centralized storehouse, large enough so that supplies and equipment now being sent direct to schools and offices could be handled in one building. Better prices would be obtained because materials could be delivered on a wholesale instead of a piecemeal basis as at present, which would help to pay for such a building in a short time.

INDEX

Absence, leaves of, for teachers, 218, 219; pupils', 196, 197; teachers' 235, 236
Achievement tests, 15, 17, 147
Adjustment, classes, 20, 45, 46, 142; schools 149, 150
Adult Education, 174-179, 180-183
After-school Centers, 91, 92, 94, 97, 126, 187-189
Agriculture, 60, 154
Americanization, 179, 180-183, 187, 252
Appointments, 212, 231, 233, 238, 241
Art, 26, 56
Associate Superintendents, See Superintendents, Board of
Athletics, 64, 73, 91-98; boys, 92-95; girls, 95-98
Attendance, Bureau of, 91, 137, 153, 155, 195-202
Banks, School 29, 148, 255
Baths, School, 190-192
Blind, Classes for the, 105, 133-135
Budget, 233, 249-256
Buildings, 35, 36, 40, 88, 172, 231, 235; annual program 252-259; number of, 260
Cardiacs, special care of, 122, 124, 127, 128

Census, 195, 200, 201
Character Education, 99-103
Citizenship Training, 25, 26, 65-69, 99, 180, 182
Civil Service, Municipal, 211, 216, 232, 234, 260, 261
Classes, size of, 17
Clubs and student organizations, 46, 47, 64, 66, 67, 68, 69, 171
Commercial courses, 41, 58, 161, 168
Community Centers, 187-189
Construction and Maintenance, Bureau of, 11, 25, 256-259
Continuation Schools, 70, 162-173, 202, 244, 245
Course of Study, continuation school, 166, 167, 168, 169; elementary school, 21-28, 32, 33; evening school, 174-178; high school, 54-61; junior high school, 41-44; kindergarten, 8; physical education, 87; training school, 206-208; ungraded class, 145; vocational, 71-75
Cripples, care of, 122, 123, 124, 125-127
Dalton Plan, 32, 62, 69, 73, 124, 167
Deaf, School for, 130-132
Deans, in high school, 62, 63
Dental Inspection, 84, 85, 90

[265]

Detention Schools, 151, 152
Directors and Assistant Directors, 240, 247
District Superintendents, 13, 235, 239, 240
Education, Board of, 30, 212, 218, 219, 229-262
Elementary Schools, regular, 12-37; evening, 174, 175; vacation, 159, 160
Estimate, Board of, 229, 230, 232, 249-254, 258
Evening Schools, 162, 174-179, 244, 245
Examiners, Board of, 91, 92, 211-217, 231, 232, 242
Experimental Schools, 13, 14, 21, 24, 25
Extension Activities, 79, 184-192
Finance, Bureau of, 250, 255, 256
Foreign, classes, 17, 18, 20, 180-183; languages, 42, 61, 152, 206
Gardens, 27, 28, 161
Grading, by ability, 13, 14, 15, 17, 61, 62
Health, Department of, 64, 79-86, 90, 171, 191, 199, 201
Health and Physical Education, 64, 73, 79-98, 252; in continuation schools, 171, 172; for handicapped children, 122, 123, 128, 129; in probationary schools, 148; in summer playgrounds, 190, 191
High Schools, 51-69; evening, 177, 178; vacation, 159-161
Home-making, 26, 27, 58, 59, 115

Hospital and Institutional Classes, 122-128, 156, 161
Hygiene, educational, 73, 89-91
Industrial Courses, in continuation schools, 166-167; in high schools, 55, 57, 58, 60; in junior high schools, 41, 42, 43, 44; for physically handicapped children, 120, 121, 136; in probationary schools, 148; for ungraded classes 142; in vocational schools, 70-75
Industrial Education, Advisory Board of, 244, 245
Inspectors and Assistant Inspectors, See Directors
Instruction, time schedule of, 23
Intelligence Tests, 15, 16, 17, 18, 25, 61, 138, 139, 143, 147
Junior High Schools, 30, 37, 38-50, 89, 206, 207; vacation, 159, 160, 161
Kindergarten and Kindergarten Extension, 7-11
Lectures, Bureau of 184, 187
Libraries, 29, 30, 65, 72, 73
Licenses, Teachers', 121, 213-215, 238, 239
Local school boards, 234-236
Lunches, 68, 69, 113-115
Medical examinations, for pupils, 64, 73, 79-86, 131, 139; for teachers, 222
Mentally Handicapped Children, 74, 75, 137-145
Model Schools, 205-207
Music, 26, 56, 57, 132, 136

INDEX

Nurses, School, 80–86
Open Air Classes, 128, 129
Opportunity Classes, 17, 20, 32
Parental School, 137, 153–156, 199, 200
Part-time and overcrowding, 35, 36, 81, 82, 160
Physical Training, Department of, 64, 87–89, 122, 123, 128
Physically Handicapped Children, 74, 119–136, 141, 252; in vacation schools, 161
Placement, of continuation school pupils, 169–171, 173; of handicapped children, 121, 135, 155; of vocational school pupils, 72, 73, 75
Plant Operation, Bureau of, 260, 261
Playgrounds, 94, 95, 190–192
Principals, 47, 62, 63, 241, 242
Probationary Schools, 137, 146–149
Promotion and Graduation, 13, 21, 22, 62, 226, 238
Psycho-Educational Clinic, 139–141
Rapid Advancement Classes, 17, 19, 39, 41, 42, 44, 48
Radio, use of, 32, 33, 186, 187
Reference, Research and Statistics, Bureau of, 13, 14, 21, 24, 25, 243–244, 250
Regents, Board of, 30, 225–228; examination by, 62, 159, 161, 178

Retardation; over-age pupils, 20, 42, 45, 46, 138, 155, 160; also see Ungraded Classes
Retirement System, Teachers', 220–222, 231, 256
Salaries, 230, 231, 249, 252
Sight Conservation, classes for, 84, 135, 136
Speech Improvement, 129, 130
State Commissioner of Education, 225, 227, 228, 230
State Department of Education, 225–228, 230
Superintendent of Schools, 195, 201, 211, 215, 231, 235–239, 243, 250, 253
Superintendents, Board of, 30, 212, 219, 232, 236, 237–243, 251, 253, 254, 257
Supplies, Bureau of, 30, 261–263
Swimming Pools, 96, 97, 190–192
Teachers, of adult day classes, 182; assignment of, 241, 242; associations, 218, 245–248; in continuation schools, 170, 172, 173; Council, 245, 246; examination of, 211–217; extension courses for, 218; of handicapped classes, 121, 129, 131; home teachers, 125, 126, 127; leaves of absence, 218, 219; requirements, 50, 103, 208, 212; retirement system, 220–222; of swimming, 192; trade, 57, 72, 75, 168, 177; training schools for, 91, 130, 205–210

[267]

Textbooks, 29, 30, 65, 72, 238, 242
Training Schools, 91, 130, 205–210
Transportation, 122, 123, 134, 262
Ungraded classes, Department of, 105, 137–145
Vacation Schools, 159–161
Visiting Teachers, 104–112, 137, 139, 146, 155, 172

Visual Instruction, 32–35, 91
Vocational, courses for shop-work, 27, 43, 44; evening schools, 175–177; guidance, 48, 49, 155, 164–166; day schools, 43, 44, 70–75, 252
Working papers, 195, 201, 202

PUBLIC EDUCATION ASSOCIATION

Founded
1895

OF THE CITY OF NEW YORK
8 WEST 40TH STREET

Incorporated
1899

THE PUBLIC EDUCATION ASSOCIATION was organized "to study the problems of public education, investigate the conditions of the common and corporate schools, stimulate public interest in the schools, and to propose from time to time such changes in their organization, management or educational methods as may seem necessary or desirable." It is an independent organization which, coöperating wherever possible with the authorities, enables citizens to make their combined influence intelligently effective for the advancement of the public schools. It supplies reliable information on current educational problems, and demonstrates new ways of adjusting the schools to the needs of the individual child.

The work of the Association falls into two main divisions: its general work in connection with current school problems, and its special projects and demonstrations to effect changes in existing procedure.

In conducting its general work, it maintains an informal information service on school affairs, holds conferences and public meetings and issues a bi-weekly bulletin entitled "The Public and the Schools," in which it expresses its views upon matters of administration and legislation of immediate importance affecting the public schools.

During its three decades of service to public education, it has not only worked actively for many of the modern developments which have been initiated by the schools themselves, but has conducted several experiments and demonstrations under its own auspices. Among these now in operation may be noted the following:

1. The establishment of visiting teacher work in the New York schools, a type of work which it has now extended on a national basis as part of the Commonwealth Fund's program for the prevention of delinquency.

2. An experiment in adjusting the school to meet the needs of the individual child in P. S. 61, one of the largest of the New York City schools.

3. A demonstration in one of the continuation schools to work out in coöperation with the Board of Health and the school authorities a practical program for meeting the physical, mental and social needs of the working child.

4. A study of the needs of cardiac and crippled children, in order to aid the schools in discovering their aptitudes and in determining what can be done to prepare them for a normal life.

5. Guidance for boys in the city prisons by seeking the causes of their difficulties and by aiding the courts and other agencies to coöperate intelligently on a sound program for rehabilitation.

The Association welcomes to membership all who are interested in the betterment of the public schools.

PUBLIC EDUCATION ASSOCIATION
OF THE CITY OF NEW YORK

TRUSTEES

FREDERIC W. ALLEN	MRS. RAY MORRIS
LEO ARNSTEIN	ROBERT H. NEILSON
MRS. JOHN BLAIR	WM. CHURCH OSBORN
WM. M. CHADBOURNE	MISS FRANCES PERKINS
JOSEPH P. COTTON	MRS. MIRIAM SUTRO PRICE
MRS. ARTHUR M. DODGE	MRS. F. LOUIS SLADE
MRS. E. C. HENDERSON	PERCY S. STRAUS
CHARLES P. HOWLAND	FREDERICK STRAUSS
DR. FRANK M. McMURRY	MRS. JOSEPH R. SWAN
OGDEN L. MILLS	HENRY W. TAFT

MRS. WM. G. WILLCOX

OFFICERS AND EXECUTIVE STAFF

President
JOSEPH P. COTTON

Vice-President
MISS MARTHA L. DRAPER

Honorary Vice-President
MRS. SCHUYLER VAN RENSSELAER

Treasurer
WILLIAM B. NICHOLS

Director
HOWARD W. NUDD

Assistant Directors
MARION CURTISS KINNEY
JOSEPHINE CHASE

Visiting Teacher Executive
JANE F. CULBERT

EXECUTIVE COMMITTEE

MRS. MIRIAM SUTRO PRICE, *Chairman*

MRS. CARL A. L. BINGER	MRS. SAMUEL LEWISOHN
JOSEPH P. COTTON	WILLIAM B. NICHOLS
MISS MARTHA LINCOLN DRAPER	G. H. PULSIFER
CLYDE FURST	KENNETH SIMPSON
MRS. E. C. HENDERSON	MRS. WM. B. OLMSTED, JR.
ALFRED JARETZKI, JR.	GEORGE D. STRAYER
MRS. LOUIS S. LEVY	MRS. WALKER E. SWIFT

LA
339
.N5
C49

Chase
New York at
school

016907

Printed in Dunstable, United Kingdom